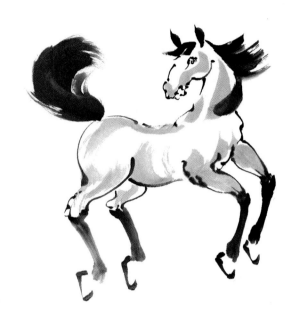

CHINESE
BRUSH PAINTING

A complete course in traditional and modern techniques

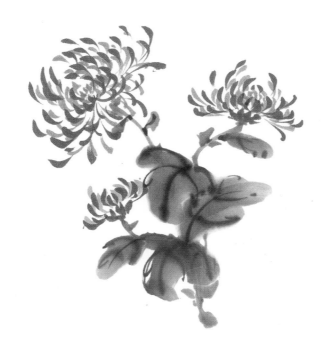

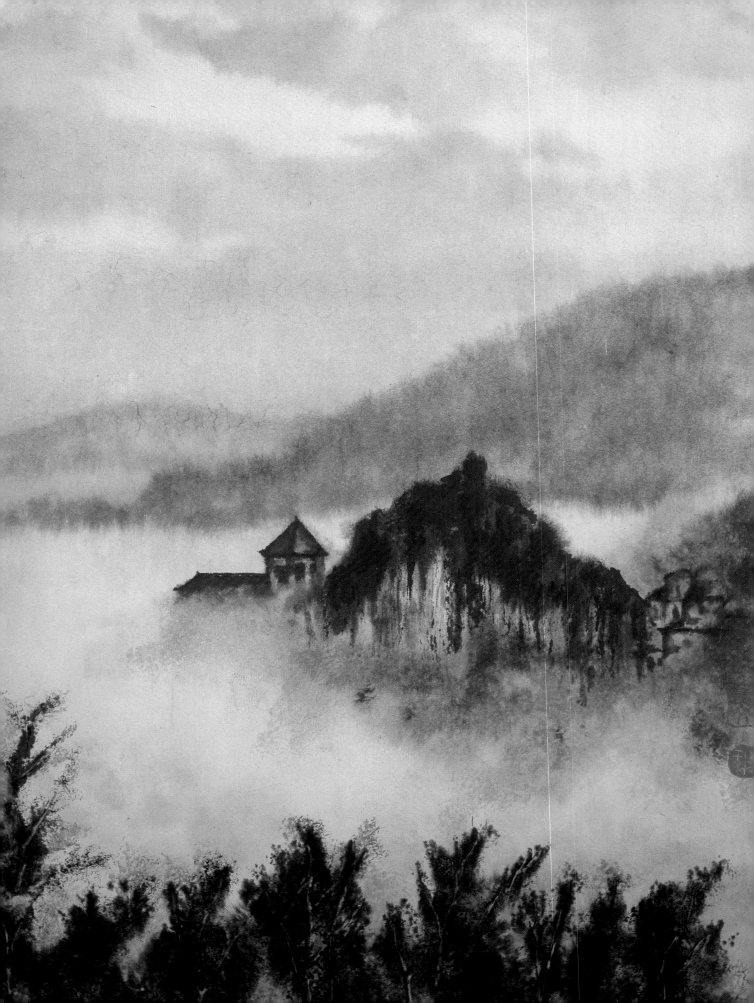

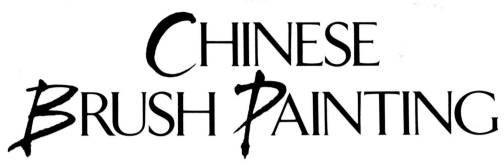

CHINESE BRUSH PAINTING

A complete course in traditional and modern techniques

JANE EVANS

WATSON-GUPTILL PUBLICATIONS

Published by Watson-Guptill Publications,
a division of Billboard Publications, Inc.
1515 Broadway, New York, NY 10036

First published in 1987 by
William Collins Sons & Co., Ltd

Copyright © 1987 by Jane Evans

Design: Lee Griffiths
Photography: Peter Lofts

Library of Congress Cataloging-in-Publication Data
Evans, Jane.
   Chinese brush painting.

   Bibliography: p.
   Includes index.
   1. Ink painting, Chinese—Technique.   2. Ink
painting—Technique.   I. Title.
ND2068.E93   1987   751.42′51   87-2047
            ISBN 0-8230-0632-8

Color reproduction by Bright Arts, Hong Kong
Printed and bound in Hong Kong
by South China Printing Co.

CONTENTS

Acknowledgments

First of all I must thank my teacher, Professor Chen Bing Sun, for giving me such an excellent grounding in Chinese brush painting. I should also like to say thank you to my own students, past and present, particularly Sheena Davis, for their interest and suggestions.

The following people very kindly loaned paintings as examples for the book: Miss E. J. Bagguley, Dr. and Mrs. A. Butterworth, Dr. and Mrs. C. Cherry, Mr. and Mrs. C. Cole, Mr. and Mrs. R. E. Davis, and Mrs. P. Hammersley.

Finally, I must thank my family for their support. Thanks are particularly due to my husband for his continual help—without his persistent encouragement the book would never have been begun, let alone completed.

Note on the spelling of Chinese words and names

The Chinese have recently adopted a new style of Western transcription known as pinyin. This has largely replaced the more familiar Wade-Giles system.

With most of the Chinese words and phrases in this book I have tried to use the new spelling, if only because it gives a much clearer idea of how words are pronounced. With names, however, I have used a mixture. There seems no point in rendering the familiar in an unfamiliar form. How many people, for example, recognize Peking in its pinyin manifestation of Beijing? Similarly, with some well-known artists who are frequently mentioned in the literature on Chinese art, I have stuck to the more recognizable form. In the case of recent artists, however, I have tried to use the spelling that most often appears in print.

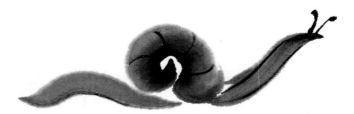

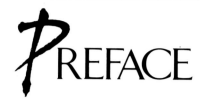REFACE

This book introduces the artist (amateur or professional) in the West to the substantial possibilities for innovation in expression offered by a mastery of Chinese brush painting techniques and attitudes.

It is intended as a comprehensive "how-to-do-it" guide for would-be brush painters and aims to take them step-by-step through the subject.

The author has been teaching Chinese brush painting for eight years and has realized the need for such a manual both as a supplement for those lucky enough to have access to classes and as a complete course for those working by themselves. Nearly everyone who starts Chinese brush painting wants to go on with it. This is partly due to the extraordinary artistic versatility of the medium, but it must also be partly because Chinese brush painting seems to exert a calming influence on its practitioners, putting them at peace with the world. It appears to have an effect somewhat similar to that of meditation.

The book aims to give students a sense of progress, there being a clear and time-honored sequence in the skills to be mastered, and definite landmarks of achievement such as are manifested in a graceful plum blossom or spirited bamboo, which they can execute after only a short time. Ends in themselves, these landmarks contribute to an ever increasing and deepening knowledge of the subject and repertoire of skills.

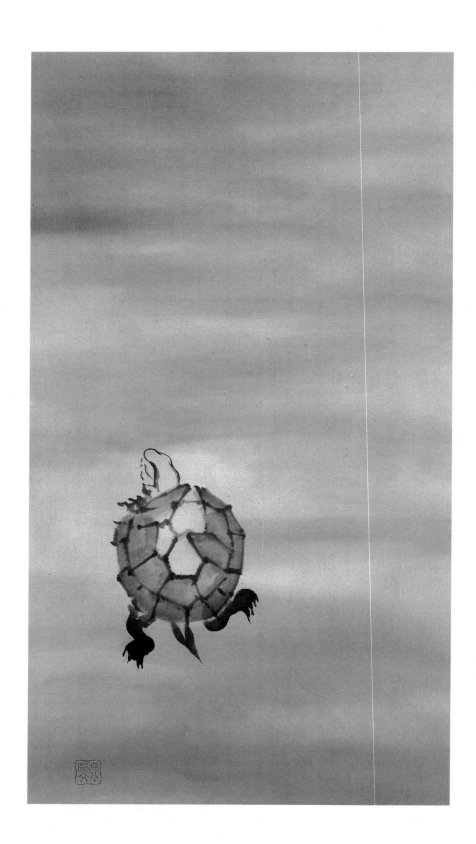

THE APPEAL OF CHINESE BRUSH PAINTING

In the West we tend to expect painters to be flamboyant, excitable, and often untidy. The Chinese painter, by contrast, is contemplative and serene, steeped in the philosophical and ethical preoccupations of his society. Perhaps this is because Chinese brush painting provides its practitioners with more than just technical skills. To learn brush painting, the would-be artist should strive not only to master the techniques but also to understand something of the philosophy and aesthetics involved. Its appeal is partly like that of such other Eastern imports as yoga and kung fu, for it seems to provide a soothing influence brought about by mastering a traditional skill through a time-honored, ritualized learning process. Japanese Sumi, or brush and ink painting, is described by Paul Siudzinski as a "meditation in ink" and this is equally applicable to Chinese painting. It scores over meditation, however, in that it can convey its calming effect to the spectator as well as to the performer. The artist also has the satisfaction of following a well-marked path to deeper understanding, with clear stages of achievement along the way.

This is not to say that Chinese painting has little to offer technically. Chinese painting materials are very versatile, far more so than their nearest Western equivalents. Chinese ink is capable of an endless variety of shades and depths of black and gray. The

---

Turtle. *The use of space and the gentle tones of the wash give this painting a peaceful atmosphere.*

color pigments combine the best properties of watercolor and those of tempera, having the transparency of the former and the permanence of the latter. The brushes, too, are almost infinitely adaptable. A good wolf-hair brush can hold considerably more paint or ink than its Western counterpart. This allows you to load it with up to three tones or colors at once so that you can, for example, complete a plant without having to go back to your palette for more color. This helps to achieve spontaneity and unity. Regardless of its size, a good brush will enable you to draw a fine line and, if spread appropriately, will give you a number of "split-brush" and "feather" strokes that a Western sable brush would resist. Horse-hair and goat-hair brushes create special effects that no Western brush can duplicate. Chinese paper comes in several qualities, some more absorbent than others. Even the least absorbent feels like a blotter to an artist accustomed to watercolor paper, but once control of the absorbency is mastered, there is a multitude of effects to be achieved with the different kinds of paper.

Westerners are sometimes put off by the thought of the effort needed to master the disciplined technique demanded by Chinese painting. You will not find yourself becoming impatient because you will progress steadily from one subject to another. You master the plum blossom, for example, before you move on to bamboo, and you must master bamboo before you move on to orchids. Thus your progress is punctuated by the acquisition of specific skills and the creation of pleasing pictures. Over a period of time you will find you have built up a store of technical knowledge that will enable you to tackle any subject. Far more than with any other painting technique, such as oil or watercolor, you will enjoy a sense of development and progress as you study. This feeling will never leave you, however long you brush paint.

The Western student brought up to believe in the importance of freedom of expression might worry that the emphasis on correct technique will lead to loss of artistic originality. This is felt particularly in the case of Chinese painting because it is traditionally learned by carefully copying the works of established artists. Indeed, the problem has not gone unnoticed by the Chinese themselves. As long ago as the seventeenth century Chieh Tzu Yüan Hua Chuan, in *The Mustard Seed Garden Manual of Painting*, stated, "If you aim to dispense with method, learn method. If you aim at facility, work hard. If you aim for simplicity, master complexity." Just as a good driver does not think about changing gears, when you have fully mastered the control of ink, brush, and paper so that it has become almost subconscious, you will be released from worry about your technical performance and be able to express yourself fully.

Even in the West, it is only in recent years that method and technique have become suspect elements in the pursuit of good art. In the past, painters studied under masters and copied their works assiduously. Today it is mainly in the visual arts that we worry that originality may be smothered by technique. No one suggests that ballet dancers should not learn the individual steps; it is the way the steps are performed and put together that determines the merit of a dancer's performance. Brush strokes are the dance steps of painting and composition its choreography.

Learning by copying is especially useful for people not brought up in the East. Not only do Chinese art students have the advantage of having been taught to write using brush, ink, paper, and even many of the brush strokes, they have also been brought up with Chinese paintings and have absorbed a feeling for composition and color in the same way that we in the

West have become familiar with Leonardo, Renoir, and Picasso. By copying from Chinese paintings, Western students can not only better appreciate the techniques and brush strokes used, but also begin to develop a feeling for composition and color that will stand them in good stead when they produce their own "original" works.

This does not mean that this method of learning has no drawbacks; indeed, the history of Chinese painting bears witness to these. There has been an inevitable tendency toward stylization and loss of freshness, and in the past there have been fewer innovative painters in China than in the West. However, this is no longer the case. The introduction of Western ideas and attitudes, and the revolutionary social and political upheaval in China have helped generate a wave of originality and innovation in Chinese painting.

Innovation does require effort, however. Provided you are aware of this and use the painted example as a general guide to brush strokes, color, and composition, rather than as a painting to be slavishly copied, the danger of simply learning how to copy rather than to create is not too great. Moreover, it can be totally overcome by your striving to become more observant of the things around you. Even though it is not used as a direct model, in the sense that Chinese artists do not traditionally sit in front of the objects they paint, you should be particularly aware of your environment. Watch birds; see how they are structured, how they land and take off, how they sit and stand, how they fluff up their feathers in winter. You should notice flowers, leaves, trees, and rocks; observe colors and shapes; and discover how things work.

There are plenty of precedents for Westerners in Chinese painting. In the seventeenth century, several Jesuit priests went to China to convert the people to Catholicism. Some of them stayed to become court painters. Best known among them was Giuseppe Castiglione, court painter to Emperor Chien Lung. His Chinese name was Lang Shih Ning. Later the Irish painter Chinnery was greatly influenced by Chinese painting and by his stay in China, and Van Gogh did a series of paintings in imitation of the Japanese style. In the twentieth century, several Chinese painters have started to look toward the West, and a number of those who are more innovative have studied abroad and adopted Western ideas on perspective and light.

Hopefully, you will achieve in your painting a blend of East and West. You will learn an idiom and a technique and come to grips with a philosophy and an outlook. My own teacher, Chen Bing Sun, liked to have an occasional European in his class. He believed that the union of China and Europe produced something interesting in painting. Therefore, while it is important that you absorb the principles of Chinese aesthetics as you learn to paint in the Chinese style, do not forget that you are a Westerner. By the end of this book you will have learned enough to feel free to "do your own thing." In other words, keep using your own aesthetic judgment and compositional skills, and combine them with your new techniques. Remember that the word *Chi-*

View from Diani Beach. *This picture was entirely created with Chinese brush painting techniques and materials. The spaciousness in the composition is also Chinese. Nevertheless, the overall effect is Western because of the perspective and the texturing of the sky and sea.*

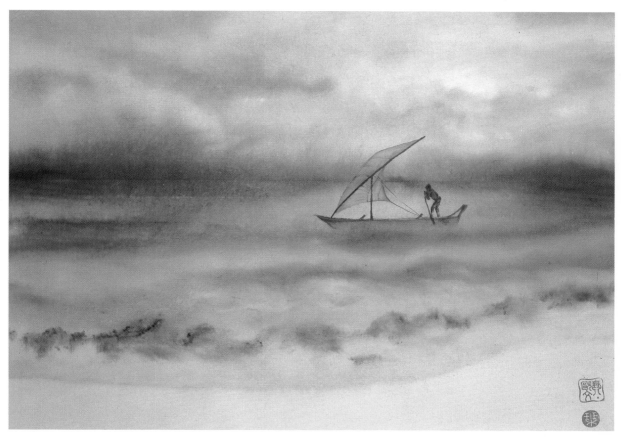

13

nese in Chinese brush painting refers to the brush, not the artist.

As a final observation to help the Western student who is interested in learning Chinese brush painting, it is perhaps worth remarking that Chinese painting lacks the self-conscious earnestness that frequently mars Western art. One of the most refreshing elements of Eastern art is its abundance of humor, as the painting below illustrates. This is not to say that Chinese painters do not take their work seriously, but they retain their ability to look at the world with a certain detached irony.

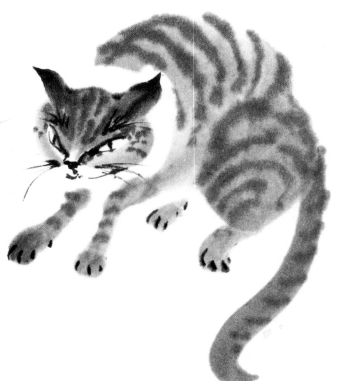

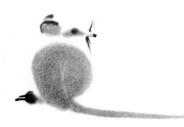

Cat and Mouse. *The humor in this painting is implied. It is left to the viewer to supply the story.*

PAINTING IN CHINESE CULTURE

It is important to be able to put what you are learning into its appropriate cultural perspective. If you know, for example, a little about the philosophical foundations of Chinese painting, you will find it easier to appreciate what qualities you should strive for and why. This book is intended to provide a practical course of instruction for the would-be brush painter; it is not an account of the history and philosophy of Chinese painting. However, this chapter attempts to provide some essential background while making no pretense at being a definitive guide. There are many excellent books available on these topics, and the bibliography at the end of this book lists a few of them.

Unlike Europe, China can claim a continuous cultural heritage going back to before 2000 B.C. The Chinese have displayed a remarkable talent for making invaders conform to Chinese cultural norms, in contrast to Europe where it was generally the invaded who succumbed to the mores, language, and institutions of the invaders. With the possible exception of the Mongols, whom they expelled after a comparatively short period, the Chinese have succeeded in Sinofying their foreign overlords, who usually made use of Chinese institutions and adopted Chinese cultural values. In fact, the invaders often became enthusiastic upholders and promoters of Chinese traditions, especially in the fields of art and literature.

It is now thought that the Chinese were using brushes for painting and writing long before the dawn of recorded Chinese history. Neolithic pottery shows clear evidence of brushwork designs, though the patterns are simple. From the sixteenth to the tenth centuries B.C., during the Shang dynasty, ideograms began to appear and evolve, although they were probably invented even earlier. There were certainly wall paintings in existence during the Zhou dynasty (c. 1000–200 B.C.) and evidence of full-fledged brushwork is abundant from the Han dynasty (c. 200 B.C.–A.D. 200) onward. Paper manufacture began during the first century, and before then there were surely silk and tomb paintings.

The history of painting in China is thus a very long one. It is also very complex. There is a tendency in the West to think of Chinese painting as homogeneous, rather like Impressionism or Italian Renaissance painting. In fact, of course, a comparable field of study would be the entire range of European painting from the Greeks and Romans to the present day, taking in all the periods of Spanish, French, Italian, German, Dutch, and English painting along the way. At any one time in China there were as many different styles of painting being produced as there were in the whole of Europe.

It is nevertheless possible to trace two broad themes or movements in Chinese painting. These are often referred to as the Academic and the Literary schools, although *school* is a misleading term in this context. In Europe it is normally applied to a group of painters such as the Pre-Raphaelites. China, too, has had move-

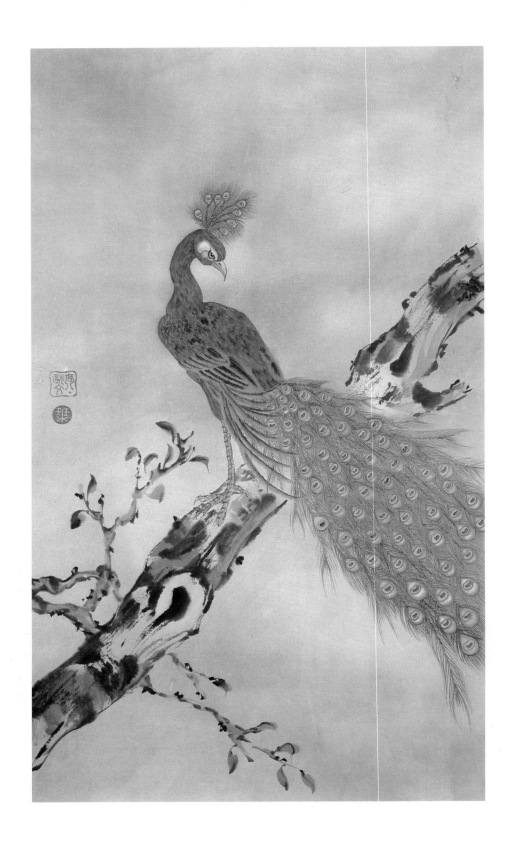

Peacock. *This is a typical example of a painstaking* gongbi *painting. Peacocks are sometimes thought to be unlucky in the West, but in the Far East they are a symbol of good fortune.*

ments and schools of painters in this European sense, but in addition all Chinese painting has tended to conform to one or the other of two major traditions, which have transcended and outlived the schools. These traditions can still be found in modern painting. You will be shown how to paint in both these ways in the later part of this book.

During the Han dynasty most painters were probably humble artisans working anonymously for a feudal lord and regarded as fairly low down on the social scale. However, it seems that a different class of Academic painters who enjoyed a much higher social status began to emerge toward the end of the Han, and the tradition of Academic painting, or Huan Hua Pai, has continued almost uninterrupted until the

present. It has been the style of court painters throughout the dynasties, has varied little through the ages, and has its modern proponents today. Described as *gongbi hua*, which can be translated as "fine style painting," it is painstaking and detailed, requiring a clean line and skillful color blending. The color is added as tinting and does not usually form a key element or contribute to the expression of the painting. Every brush stroke is precise. Pictures done in this style tend to be formal and elaborate and take time to produce.

The other main tradition in Chinese painting is the Literary school, or Wen Jen Hua Pai. Most of today's painters in China and outside it can probably best be seen as descendants of this school. It is characterized by the *xieyi hua*, which can roughly be translated as "to write an idea." It was

Bird in the Snow. *A* xieyi *painting in which the bird is painted in a few expressive strokes.*

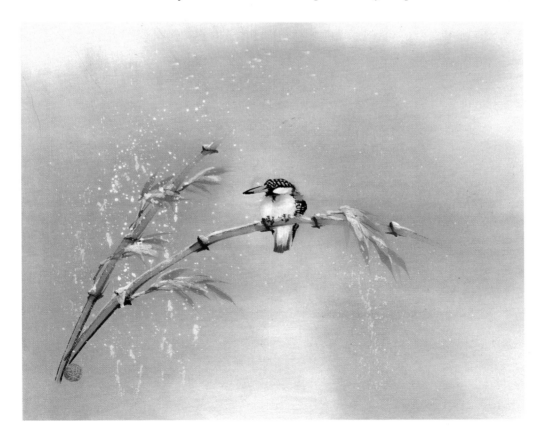

undoubtedly developed to liberate artists from *gongbi*, and its aim is to depict as much as possible in the smallest number of bold strokes. Its style is simplified and free— vital expression is more important than the mere rendering of form. *Xieyi* is much more difficult to master than *gongbi*. A *xieyi* painting should be completed "in one breath"; in other words, it should be done in one sitting so that the life force is not broken. The term used to describe this rhythmic vitality or harmony with the *chi* is *chi yuen*. As all natural things have an inner spirit, the *chi*, they also have *yuen*, which is the flowing vitality that expresses the *chi*.

A *xieyi* painting should be lively, the brush strokes bold and firm. It should show rhythm and fluidity. A *xieyi* painting must not be merely technically accomplished, however. It can be a compliment to a painting to describe it as *chuo*, or awkward, because this distinguishes it from *chiao*, which means dextrous and clever but lacking in feeling. *Xieyi* paintings should be spontaneous and exciting to look at. A painting should represent the artist's distillation and comprehension of reality rather than be simply an actual representation of it. It should embody his perception of the underlying true nature of his subject.

Most of the innovative influences in Chinese painting have come from the Literary school; even today painters are able to absorb Western ideas and techniques and yet produce works of art that are part of an unbroken tradition of expressive Chinese painting stretching back at least as far as the critic Hsieh Ho in the fifth century.

No survey of Chinese painting would be complete without mention of the Lingnam school, which grew up in Canton at the end of the nineteenth century. It was founded by Gao Jianfu, who had studied Nanga painting in Japan and who was a political follower of Sun Yatsen. With his brother Gao Qifeng and a friend, Chen Shuren, Gao founded the New National Painting after the 1911 revolution. They introduced contemporary subject matter and used realistic techniques when depicting animals and birds. They also used light effects, shading, and perspective. Today the largest group of Lingnam painters is in Hong Kong, and the most influential artist is Zhao Shaoang, a pupil of Gao Qifeng. Most modern Lingnam painters concentrate on bird and flower paintings, and they break with tradition in their use of varied, bright colors.

The history of painting in China is closely allied to the history of thought. Chinese painting is not merely a visual art; it is also a literary and philosophical one. The real roots of Chinese painting can be traced to three philosophies: Taoism, Confucianism, and Buddhism. Lao Tse, the founder of Taoism, was born in 571 B.C. He was a contemporary of Confucius. Lao believed that men's desires and ambitions were the causes of social unrest and turmoil. He advocated withdrawal and noninterference in the affairs of others. Taoism does not have gods and spirits, and there are no benevolent or malevolent beings controlling nature. Lao believed that "Heaven and earth are not kind. They treat everything as straw dogs." Tao is the vital life force in all things, and *chi* is its manifest form. The Yin and the Yang are the complementary positive and negative forces, the union of which is essential for creation. From this union came heaven, earth, and all natural things. *Chi* is the force that harmonizes Yin and Yang. Everything has its own special characteristic coming from Tao, and all natural things must act according to their Tao; water does not act like rock, the bird does not behave like the fish.

These concepts underlie the fundamental principles of most Chinese brushwork, and their embodiment in painting is in turn an expression of Taoist ideals.

It is Taoism that gives Chinese painting its use of space as a positive compositional element. To the Taoist, space is as important as nonspace. Lao stated, "Thirty spokes support the hub of a wheel; because of the space within the hub, the cart is able to move. Vessels may be made of clay; it is the space inside that makes them useful. Build a room with a door and windows; it is the space through the door and windows which is useful."

Taoism also stresses the virtue of simplicity, a tenet that has greatly influenced Chinese life in general and art in particular. The artist keeps his subject simple, trying for a simple effect and for economy of line

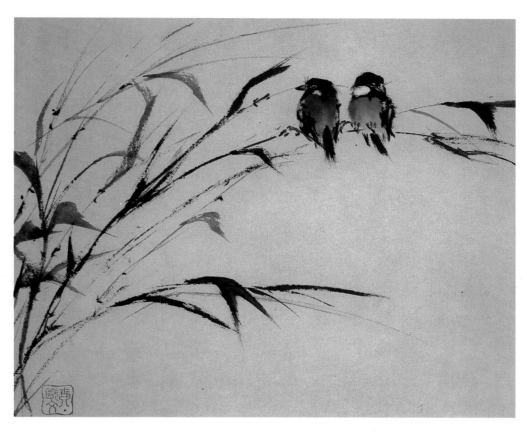

Birds in the Wind. *This painting of two small* xieyi *birds shows how space is used as an important compositional element.*

and color. Subdued color is aesthetically pleasing. In Taoist thinking, man's place in the scheme of things is unimportant and artists reflect this by concentrating on natural themes and landscapes, relegating figures to minor roles in these. Taoism is particularly relevant to Literary painting values. The Taoists believed that it was possible for art to get in the way of man's relationship with nature and therefore the artist should not strive to achieve beauty at the expense of expression.

A Chinese painting is not representational in the Western sense. It is not a portrayal of a particular bird, animal, or flower, but rather a representation of the spirit, or *chi*, of its subject expressed at a moment in time. There is an apocryphal tale of a European painter and a Chinese painter being

given three days to produce a picture of a duck. They went to the duck pond and sat on a bench. The European spent two of his three days making detailed sketches of individual ducks before spending the third day, still by the pond, producing a portrait of one particular duck on the pond. The Chinese sat and watched the ducks for two and a half days. On the last afternoon he returned to his studio and painted his picture. It was not a portrait of any one specific duck but expressed what he felt was the *chi* of ducks in general.

Confucius, who lived from 551 to 479 B.C., took a different view of the world from Lao Tse. He advocated taking an active part in life and was himself energetic in the service of his country. Confucius' teachings have had a profound effect on Chinese culture; they have been widely studied and promulgated, and their influence can be seen in sculptures and monuments, as well as in paintings.

Confucius placed great importance on

19

high ethical standards. He stressed duty as the path to harmony. Sincerity of thought and action was the aim of education and knowledge. In Confucianism an artistic training helped to produce men of culture and high moral standards, although Confucius himself did not regard art as important. Art merely served to illustrate the need for order and harmony in life. And he did not even accord painting the status of an art; he saw it as a craft. He was more concerned with the influence of music, which he regarded with suspicion. From Confucianism, however, Chinese painting gained a great deal of its formality and adherence to tradition, although Confucianism cannot be said to have contributed originality and spontaneity to Chinese art.

The Buddhist religion was introduced into China in the reign of Han Ming Ti, who ruled from A.D. 58 to 75. With it came Buddhist painting and sculpture. Chan, or Zen Buddhism, was established during the seventh century. Zen emphasizes the attainment of nirvana through meditation and has had a great influence on Chinese art. From Buddhism, Chinese painting acquired its meditative mood and the emphasis on the use of black ink. Buddhism also reinforced the importance of simplicity and required painting to be contemplative rather than merely decorative.

All three of these philosophical influences have been at work over the centuries. It is usually possible to detect elements of each of them in a painting, even if one predominates.

By now you should have an idea of the very rich heritage of Chinese painting, and perhaps your appetite has been whetted to try your hand at the very satisfying, practical application of the art.

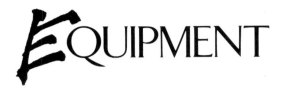QUIPMENT

Successful brush painting requires the correct materials and equipment, and an understanding of the properties of these is essential for their effective use. The Chinese refer to the Four Treasures of painting, which are the ink stick, the ink stone, the brush, and the paper. In addition to these, you will need a selection of colors, a palette

Two ink stones (one with lid), Chinese and Japanese ink sticks, two seals (chops), and a jar of seal ink.

to mix them on, and various other materials as described on page 25.

The ink stick
Chinese ink usually comes solidified into rectangular sticks made of carbon and glue. These sticks are always decorated in some way, and some are very beautifully embellished with elaborate colored pictures. Others have more simple embossed designs or a few characters in gold. Ink sticks vary in quality, some grinding down to give a very

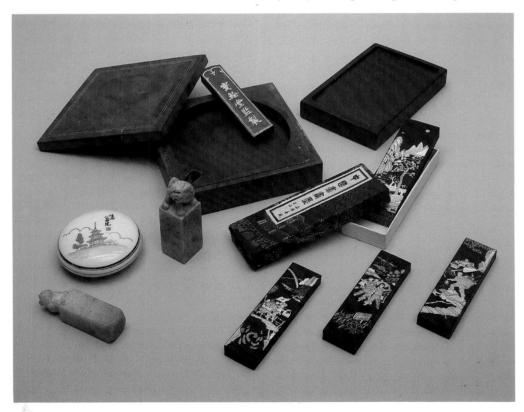

dark, brownish-black ink, others giving a grayer tone. As with most things, it pays to invest in a good-quality ink stick, which will give you a clearer, purer black than a cheap one. You can also use Japanese ink sticks, which have rounded tops and whose quality is sometimes shown by a star coding. Although it is occasionally possible to buy Chinese ink in liquid form, it is not recommended, because the act of grinding the ink before beginning to paint has a calming effect and puts you into a suitable frame of mind while simultaneously loosening your arm. In any case, some of the bottled inks contain a preservative that destroys the nonrunning properties of the ink. Japanese tubes of ink are usually more reliable in this respect.

The ink stone

The ink should be ground on an ink stone. Those available in the West are usually of two types: circular with a lid and a small hole for draining off unused ink, and rectangular with a slope at one end providing a reservoir for ground ink. Both types come in various sizes, but do not get one that is too small or you will not be able to grind enough ink at any one time.

The brush

A Chinese brush is constructed differently from a Western one. The hairs in a Western brush go down inside a metal clamp, or ferrule, which holds them in place. The head of a Chinese brush, however, is held together with adhesive, which also holds it in the top of the bamboo, wood, or bone shaft. Whereas a good Western brush springs back into its original shape after each stroke, the hair of a Chinese brush is carefully selected, graded, and arranged so that the brush can either form a fine point or be used spread out or split. A Chinese brush holds much more paint or ink than an equivalent-sized Western brush and, as already explained, can therefore be loaded with up to three tones of ink or three colors at once. No one species provides the hair for Chinese brushes: goat, rabbit, sheep, deer, weasel, pig, badger, and horse are all used. Brushes that are labeled wolf hair are actually made of sable or weasel.

There are three main categories of brush:

resilient, soft, and coarse. All three come in a full range of sizes. Because of the way it is made, any good resilient brush, regardless of its size, can be used to draw a fine, delicate line. Resilient brushes are used for almost all Chinese painting. They are often made of weasel hair and are light brown in color. Because they are the most versatile and widely used brushes, you should equip yourself with at least three: an orchid brush (that is, one the ideal size for painting orchids), a plum blossom brush, and a bamboo brush. The orchid brush head is thin and about ½ inch long; the plum blossom brush head is the same length but twice as fat; and the bamboo brush head should be about 1 inch long and firmly padded.

The soft and the coarse brushes are used for special effects. At first you will not use them, although later you may find you want to invest in different sizes of these, too. Soft brushes are usually made of goat or sheep hair and are white in color. They are particularly useful for freestyle painting when a soft, blurred effect is required, as in the breast of a bird or the leaf of a lotus. The coarse brushes are made of horsehair and are dark brown. They are helpful for successful Lingnam-style painting and are used to achieve the ragged effect and bold strokes needed. Since they are expensive, you can substitute large, cheap Japanese brushes, which produce a somewhat similar effect and are available at most art supply stores.

You will also need a wash brush and a mounting brush. Wash brushes are made of goat's hair, are flat, and have bristles about ½ inch long. A 1-inch-wide brush is ideal; anything wider is rather unwieldy. A mounting brush looks like a wash brush, but its bristles are slightly firmer and longer.

It is vital to buy good-quality brushes. It is not easy, however, to determine how good a brush is by looking at it in the store, because all brushes are sized to keep them in shape before use. Cheap brushes, which look perfectly good when bought, can turn out, after they are soaked, to be padded with inferior-quality hair in the center. Unfortunately, though perhaps not unnaturally, stores are not well disposed toward customers who try to part the hairs to make sure the quality is consistent throughout.

Luckily, however, price is usually a reliable indicator of quality, so you should always buy the most expensive brush of its size.

You must soak the brush in water thoroughly to remove the sizing before using it for the first time. Once you have soaked a brush, you should never recap it. In fact, some of the better-quality brushes are sold without caps, which can damage the bristles. Brushes should always be washed in water after use and hung point downward to dry; some have small loops on the end of the handles for this purpose. Brushes not in use should be rolled in a slatted bamboo mat.

The silk or paper

Chinese painting is done on silk or on *shuan* paper. *Chuan*, or silk, is sized with a solution of alum and glue to make *hua chuan*, or picture silk. Using silk gives a translucent quality to detailed *gongbi* work and enhances the use of color. Provided the amount of color used is properly controlled so that the paint does not run along the threads of the cloth, a subtle blending is possible because the paint does not soak in as it does on paper. Silk is less suitable for *xieyi* painting and is almost never used for calligraphy.

The *chih*, or paper, for Chinese painting and calligraphy is usually called rice paper in English, although only a few papers are actually made of rice straw. Others are made from reeds, hemp, mulberry, bamboo, grass, and cotton. Bamboo pulp is generally thought to make the best paper for painting and is the kind most commonly available in the West. It is known as *shuan chih* and comes in various thicknesses and qualities, treated with variable amounts of sizing. The more alum used, the less absorbent the paper becomes and the easier the control of the ink. To an artist accustomed to Western watercolor paper, however, even the most heavily sized sheet of *shuan* feels like a blotter at first. The various absorbencies are used to create different effects. Work done on unsized paper must be of the "in-one-breath" style, whereas color blending and detailed work are best done on well-sized *shuan*.

Japanese papers, particularly *kozo* and *moriki*, are suitable for brush painting and are readily available in art supply stores.

Grass paper, cotton paper, and hemp paper are difficult to find in the West. Newsprint is a cheap medium for practicing brush strokes at the beginning, although its limitations become apparent fairly rapidly. For example, it is difficult to achieve tonal variation with the ink on newsprint, which tends to make even the blackest ink look wishy-washy, and it also only absorbs paint on immediate impact, causing any surplus paint on the brush to puddle. In addition, newsprint cannot take a wash or be mounted. It can be very frustrating for a beginner to achieve a satisfying painting of a plum branch, only then to realize that it cannot be mounted and framed.

Colors

Traditionally, Chinese colors are made from mineral and vegetable pigments. A beginner will need a basic palette of about seven colors: indigo, rattan yellow, burnt sienna, rouge, vermilion, light mineral green, and white. Later you can expand your color range as you like. It is possible to buy boxed tubes of Chinese painting color (not to be confused with Chinese oil color or Chinese watercolor) in Chinese supermarkets, bookstores, and gift shops. These are reasonably priced, but the box contains twelve colors of which you will use only six with any frequency. As the tubes are small, these six will soon run out. It is better to try to obtain solid colors, which are occasionally sold in Chinese shops and are available from large art supply stores. Apart from yellow, Chinese solid colors come either as cakes in ceramic dishes or as small chips of color in boxes. These chips should be put into a dish and dissolved with hot water to form a cake. Some mineral colors come in powdered form, but are not recommended because mixing them is quite complicated. The yellow, which is solidified rattan sap and is slightly poisonous, comes in rough lumps of variable sizes. To use it, simply moisten a lump with a wet brush. You should eschew the very expensive boxed sets of color sticks that can often be bought in art stores selling Eastern materials. Not only are these sticks costly, but you would also need a great many ink stones to grind them on.

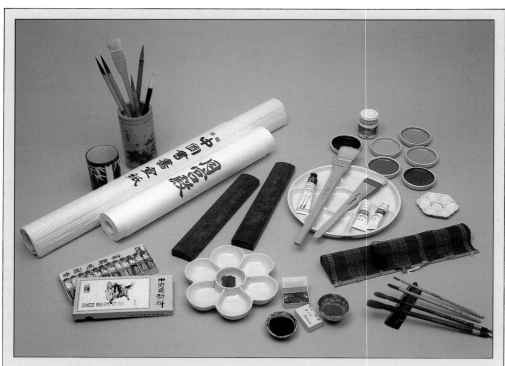

Chinese brush painting equipment.

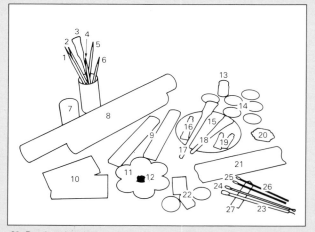

1 Horsehair brush (unused)
2 Horsehair brush (unused)
3 Japanese wash brush
4 Japanese Inscribe brush (unused)
5 Resilient brush, bamboo size
   (unused)
6 Medium soft brush (unused)
7 Water jar
8 Paper
9 Pair of paperweights
10 Box of Chinese painting colors
11 Palette
12 Lump of Chinese rattan yellow
13 Jar of gouache white
14 Japanese Teppachi colours
15 Palette
16 Gouache color
17 Mounting brush
18 Chinese wash brush
19 Gouache colors
20 Small palette
21 Bamboo mat brush holder
22 Chinese colors: chips in boxes and
   diluted chips in bowls

23 Bamboo brush
24 Plum blossom brush
25 Orchid brush
26 Small orchid brush
27 Brush rest

Most art supply stores sell Japanese colors, which come in flat ceramic dishes and provide a very practical solution to the supply problem. Unfortunately, some of the colors are not the same as the Chinese ones, so, for example, you will have to substitute cadmium yellow for the rattan and alizarin crimson for the red.

You can use ordinary Western watercolors to practice with, although pictures painted with these cannot take a wash or be mounted. Poster or gouache white makes a satisfactory substitute for Chinese lead white. Other gouache colors also work well if you cannot obtain the Chinese or Japanese pigments. They have fixing qualities similar to Chinese colors, but lack their transparency. This comparative lack of delicacy does not necessarily matter; indeed, it can be an advantage in the kind of freestyle paintings that use many bright colors.

Palettes

Also necessary is a white china palette, preferably one divided into fairly large sections. Most watercolor palettes sold in art stores have very small subdivisions, which are not practical for loading sequences of color on a brush or for mixing washes. Some Chinese stores sell painting dishes about 8 inches in diameter and divided into sections. Even better, however, in that they are larger, have different-sized sections, and are cheaper, are fondue plates sold in housewares departments. You should avoid colors and patterns on these, though, since they make ink and color tones difficult to distinguish. Empty Japanese color dishes also make useful mixing dishes.

Other necessary equipment

You will need a large, steady table at a comfortable height for working. You should also have good light, preferably daylight. In addition, you need a water jar; a roll of paper towels; a bamboo place mat for storing brushes when they are not in use; and an old towel or newspaper to put under the paper to absorb excess moisture when applying a wash. For some reason *shuan* paper, unlike your fingers, will not pick up newsprint.

Optional equipment

There are a few items of equipment that are not vital but will simplify your life or enhance your painting. Paperweights fall into this category, preferably the long, narrow Chinese ones which are sold in pairs and are specially designed for painters and calligraphers. A jar for holding brushes while they are in use is also helpful, but it should not be used as a permanent storage place because it holds the brushes upright, allowing moisture to collect at the base of the hairs and loosen the glue. You can also buy brush rests at a number of Chinese and Japanese stores. When mounting, a large table with a wipeable surface, such as Formica, simplifies the task greatly.

Your finished paintings will be very much enhanced by a chop, or seal, which it is now possible to have carved in San Francisco (see page 138). A chop is usually applied with red ink and can be made to represent a name or a suitable phrase.

Now that you have the proper tools, you are ready to begin a great adventure.

MAKING A START

While there is obviously no substitute for watching a teacher perform the brush strokes and mix the ink, this book is meant to provide the next best thing to traditional lessons in Chinese brush painting. You should regard the book as providing a course and try to master each stage before going on to the next.

The Chinese method of learning anything, be it painting or kung fu, can be broken down into three steps: watch; do; understand. You can learn by imitation and repetition until finally the *chi* flows through you and you understand. In other words, you should not worry about *why* you are doing something; its purpose will become clear in time. This book provides instructions for the watching and imitating stages; the rest is up to you.

In Chinese brush painting there is a logical sequence of learning, evolved over centuries, which will enable you to build up your repertoire of brushstrokes just as a music student builds up his repertoire of notes and scales. *The Mustard Seed Garden Manual of Painting* has advice for the would-be painter on the need for being methodical:

He who is learning to paint . . . should begin to study the basic brushstroke technique of one school. He should be sure that he is learning what he set out to learn, and that heart and hand are in accord. After this, he may try miscellaneous brushstrokes of other schools and use them as he pleases. He will then be at the stage when he himself may set up the matrix in the furnace and, as it were, cast in all kinds of brushstrokes of whatever schools and in whatever proportion he chooses. He himself may become a master and the founder of a school. At this

later stage, it is good to forget the classifications and to create one's own combinations of brushstrokes. At the beginning, however, the various brushstrokes should not be mixed.

Even Fang Zhaoling, who is one of the most innovative Chinese painters working today, exhibiting in the United States, Great Britain, Hong Kong, and China, recognizes that it was vital for her to have a thorough grounding in basic brushwork. She spent ten years studying under Zhao Shaoang of the Lingnam school before she felt the need to break away and the confidence to express herself by creating her own style.

The best way to learn is to practice each stage thoroughly. You must be patient, however, and prepared to work hard. Only by constant practice will you learn to paint with confidence and ease.

Do not let yourself become discouraged during these early stages. At first you may feel that you will never progress beyond the basics, but it is vital to be most thorough at the beginning or you will never achieve the facility and effortlessness that are the hallmarks of a successful brush painting. Eventually you will be rewarded by finding that later lessons take less time to learn. In any case, the learning process is a continuous one; my own teacher claimed he was still learning after fifty years.

One of my students related a no-doubt apocryphal story she had heard about a man who went to a famous Chinese painter to commission a picture. He was told to come back a year later, and this he did. On seeing his customer, the painter got out paper, brush, ink, and ink stone; he ground

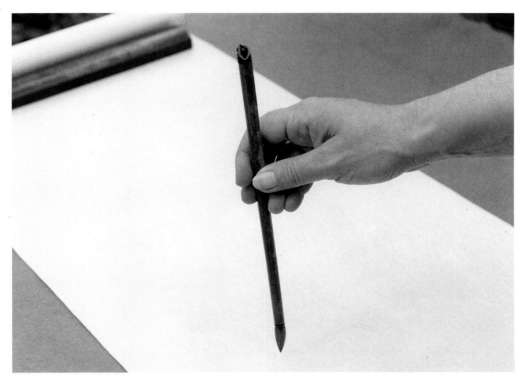

The correct way to hold the brush.

the ink and in a few strokes completed a painting that was exactly what was required. The customer, mystified, inquired about the need for a year's delay. Without a word, the artist got up from his seat at the table and opened a cupboard in a corner of the room. It was full of practice versions of the painting on the table.

Before you begin to paint, there are several general points you should always remember. First of all, try to be in a calm and contemplative frame of mind. Take time preparing your materials; make sure that your physical environment is soothing; shut yourself away in a quiet corner (the kitchen table with children underfoot is not recommended). Enjoy the process of getting ready to paint before you actually start the painting itself.

You should always strive for sureness and boldness in your brush strokes. Even when the subject of your painting is small and detailed, the individual brush strokes should be deft and certain. This may result in somewhat rough results at first, but you

should remember that the Chinese admire paintings that are *chuo*, or awkward, and are scathing about those that are dextrous but lack feeling. In time you will gain control over the brush and will be able to make it do what you want without losing any spontaneity.

When you are learning by copying, it is important not to be too slavish about it. A common mistake is to continue to look at what you are copying while actually painting. This results in a hesitant line. You should look at the subject before putting brush to paper and then reproduce an impression of it from memory. To help you achieve spontaneity and feeling in your painting, you should always use the largest brush that is practical for any given subject. This encourages you to use fewer strokes.

Holding the brush correctly

A Chinese brush is held quite differently from a Western one. It should always be held as upright as possible, between the thumb and the middle finger with the other three fingers providing guidance rather than support, the index finger in front of

27

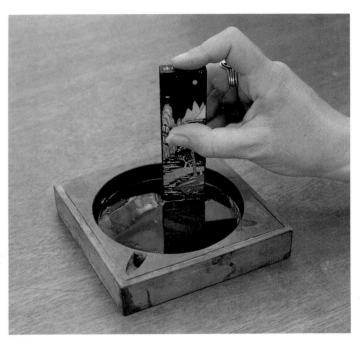

Use a circular motion to grind the ink.

---

the ink stone and, holding the ink stick upright, grind it with circular movements until the motion leaves a dry patch on the stone. This indicates that the water has absorbed as much ink as possible. However, you should always test the ink to make sure that it is a good, rich black. Take care not to leave the ink stick upright on the stone because the moistened glue in it will cause adhesion.

Gray tones are achieved by placing a small amount of black ink on a china palette and diluting it with water to the desired shade. Some subjects require a great deal of ink, others less. It is a common fault of students to not grind enough ink and to try to stretch the ink too far by overdiluting it.

Composition

Be careful about composition. Allow yourself a piece of paper that is larger than you think you will need. This should help you to avoid a tendency some people have to make their subjects too small and therefore rather cramped. However, you must also avoid the opposite temptation, which is to fill the paper completely. Remember that space is an essential element of composition in Chinese painting. Westerners tend to worry about unused space in paintings and seem to have a distressing need to fill it, and you must learn to curb this desire when you are brush painting.

The amount of space devoted to individual subjects in this book is not necessarily indicative of the amount of practice they demand. It is simply assumed that as you progress through the course, you will acquire a certain knowledge and therefore later subjects can be dealt with in less detail.

Most lessons begin with what is often called the outline, or contour, method and then go on to present the freestyle technique. This distinction is useful for explanatory purposes, but no painting need be done exclusively in one or the other method. For example, outlined flowers will often be accompanied by freestyle leaves, or an outlined bird will be perched on a freestyle branch.

the brush and the ring and little finger keeping it upright from behind. The brush should be loosely held, not tightly gripped. For small details you may hold it fairly close to the bristles, but larger, freer strokes are done with the brush quite high up the shaft. The movement of the strokes comes from the shoulder, not the wrist, so you should make sure you are sitting or standing in a relaxed but upright position, with plenty of freedom for your shoulder to move.

Grinding the ink

It is crucial to grind your ink black enough. Nothing mars the effect of a picture so much as poor ink values. You should grind your ink stick from the bottom—which you can identify from the calligraphy or picture on the side of the stick—because the ink at the top of the stick, where you hold it, is often less dense. Some experts claim that distilled water should be used for grinding ink, but it usually is not. Put a few drops of water on the grinding surface of

PAINTING PLUM OR JADE BLOSSOMS

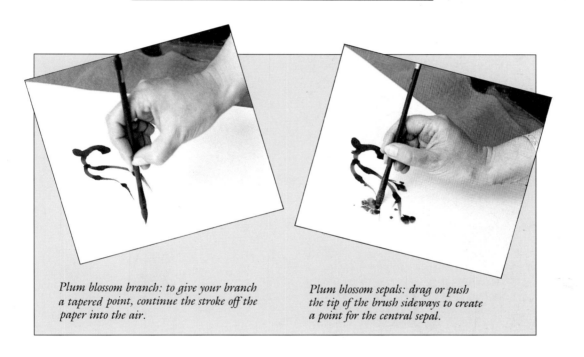

Plum blossom branch: to give your branch a tapered point, continue the stroke off the paper into the air.

Plum blossom sepals: drag or push the tip of the brush sideways to create a point for the central sepal.

Many people expect to start by painting bamboo. However, traditionally the first of the Four Friends (plum, bamboo, orchid, and chrysanthemum) attempted by students of Chinese painting is the plum or jade blossom. It is logical to begin with this because the execution of a plum blossom calls for several skills that are needed for every aspect of brush painting. For example, painting a plum blossom will require you to control the tone of your ink and the amount of moisture on your brush. In addition, you will find that the drawing of a plum blossom is greatly facilitated by holding the brush correctly, and you will therefore acquire good habits right from the beginning. You will also learn dry and wet brush techniques when doing branches and will discover the value of working quickly and deftly to obtain a spirited effect.

What is referred to as the plum or jade blossom of Chinese painting is usually the Japanese apricot. A symbol of winter, it is much admired in China. Gardeners tend the trees with care; poets extol its beauty and purity in words; and painters strive to capture its *chi* on paper. According to tradition, the blossoms themselves are the Yang

29

and the trunk and branches the Yin; the three sepals are heaven, earth, and man; and the five petals are the elements. The stamens represent the planets.

Flowers: outline method
To paint a plum blossom, first grind your ink. Then take a medium-sized plum blossom brush and with it transfer a small amount of ink to your palette. Still using the brush, add water gradually until you have a reasonable quantity of gray ink.

Rinse and dry your brush. Beginners often forget to do this, but it is very important. If you do not dry your brush, the water that has accumulated at the base of the bristles while you have been mixing your ink will run down to the tip and hamper your painting.

Using just the tip of your brush, dip it into the gray ink and gently wipe off any surplus on the side of the palette, keeping the point of the brush intact.

Holding the brush upright between the thumb and the middle finger, as shown on page 27, practice drawing slightly elliptical circles about ⅓ inch in diameter. Use even pressure and remember to keep the brush upright all the time. This will ensure that you move the whole brush rather than just tilt it, which would result in an outline of uneven thickness. If the tip of your brush inadvertently misses the paper at any point, do not attempt to go back and fill in. Simply leave the gap and let the viewer's eye supply the continuation.

When you feel you can achieve a uniform line, start joining your shapes together to build up a flower as illustrated at right. Begin with the complete petal in the center, making your taking-off point the place from which you are later going to paint the central sepal. Next, do the two petals on either side and fill in the remaining two petals.

For the stamens use black ink. Starting nearest the petal edge and working from your shoulder, do a quick flicking stroke, using just the tip of the brush. To make the stamen taper to a point, continue the stroke off the paper into the air. Start with the center stamen and always try to have either seven or nine on each flower. The pollen is dabbed on in a random manner.

The sepals are done last. Use very black ink and soak the brush with it about halfway down. The two sepals on either side are formed by placing the tip of the brush on the paper and pressing it down sideways for a moment before lifting it off cleanly. To form the one in the middle, begin in the same way, but after pressing down, you must pull the brush down or up (depending on the angle of the flower) so that it leaves a tail as it comes off the paper. A common beginner's mistake is to try to draw a comma shape with the tip of the brush. The point is actually made, not by the tip of the brush, but by the side as it comes away from the paper.

Once you have mastered this basic flower, try the varying shapes and angles known as the twelve traditional faces of the plum blossom, shown at left. With **a** and **b**, start by drawing two circles side by side, beginning and finishing each brush stroke at the bottom. Then draw in the three semicircles.

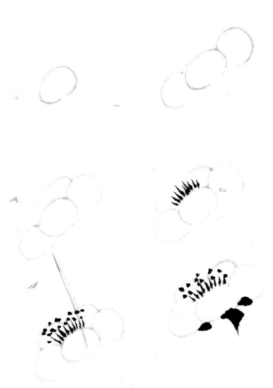

Building up a single outlined plum blossom flower.

For **c**, begin as you did for the basic flower but omit the last two petals. For **d** there are only semicircular petals and the five sepals are formed by placing the tip of the brush on the paper appropriately. Flowers **e** to **j** are all variations showing differing angles and the stamens and sepals in various positions. Remember to begin your complete petal from the point where you will join the center sepal. The buds, **k** and **l**, have slightly smaller petals than the open flowers and are somewhat egg-shaped, but the principle of painting them is the same.

Flowers: freestyle method

When you have mastered the outlined flowers, you should try a freestyle one. This looks easier but is actually more difficult than an outlined one, so do not despair if your early efforts resemble a cat's paw prints. Once again, begin with an ink stone full of very black ink. As before, take some ink and dilute it to make gray, but note that

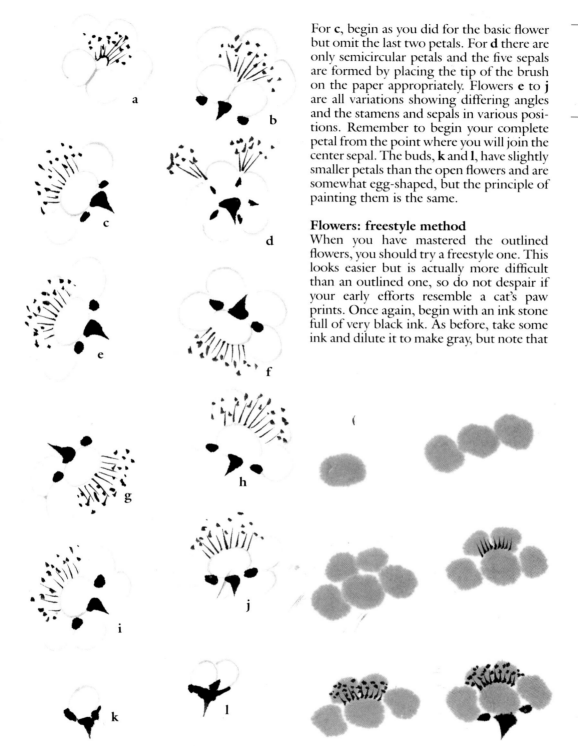

The twelve traditional faces of the plum blossom, done by the outline method.

Building up a single, freestyle plum blossom flower.

31

a

b

c

d

e

f

g

h

i

j

k

l

*The twelve traditional faces of the plum blossom,
done by the freestyle method.*

this time you will need a lot more gray ink.
Do not forget to rinse and dry your brush
after mixing.

The petals are done in the same order as
before, but they are formed as a solid shape.
First, soak your brush in the gray ink and
wipe off the excess on the side of the palette.
Holding the brush upright, place the tip on
the paper and then press down while rolling
the brush around, either completely or halfway, depending on which petal you are
doing. The tip of your brush thus forms the
center of your petal and the petal edge is
described by the heel. This needs to be done
quickly; otherwise your ink will spread too
much and the edges of your petals will be
too blurred. Try to keep your petals close
together without allowing them to merge.

The stamens, pollen, and sepals are done
in the same way as before, with very black
ink. It is best to do them before the petals
have dried so that they will blend in slightly
with the lighter ink.

Branches
Like the flowers, plum branches can be
painted using either the outline or the freestyle method. Either kind of blossom can be
used with either kind of branch. Freestyle
branches are best done while you are standing, to give your arm the freedom to move
properly.

The four examples on pages 33 and 34
illustrate various techniques used in painting plum blossom branches. For the first
figure you should grind plenty of ink and
have your brush full and fairly wet. Using
the whole brush, and without taking it off
the paper, execute each branch as quickly as
possible. Make the joints by pausing
slightly, and the thicker parts of the branch
by pressing with more of your brush. At the
end of a branch you should pull the stroke
into the air as you did for the stamens, to
give your branch a tapered point. If you
want the end of the branch to be blunt,
simply stop the stroke abruptly and lift the
brush cleanly off the paper. When your
branch is complete, add some random dabs
of very black ink to represent lichen or
moss.

The next example is worked with a
slightly drier brush. The thick main branch
is made by holding the brush sideways and

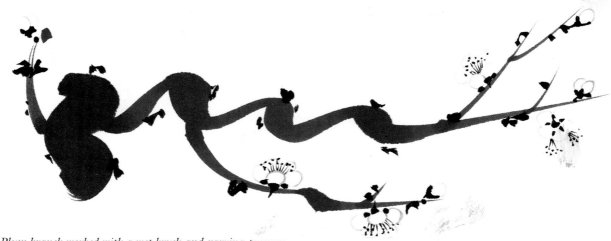

Plum branch worked with a wet brush and varying pressure.

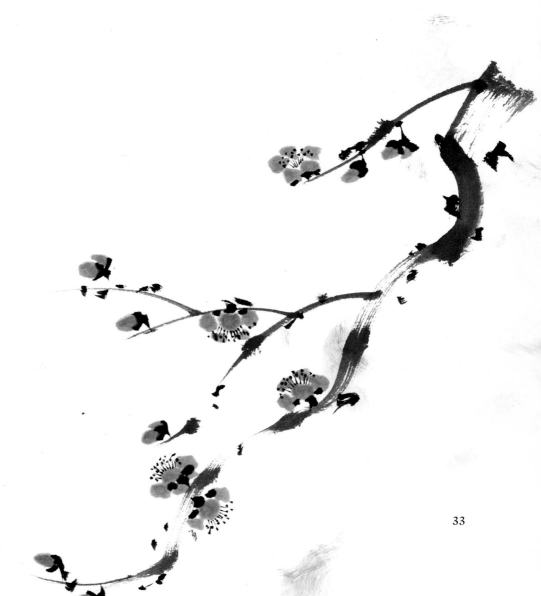

Plum branch worked with a drier brush.

33

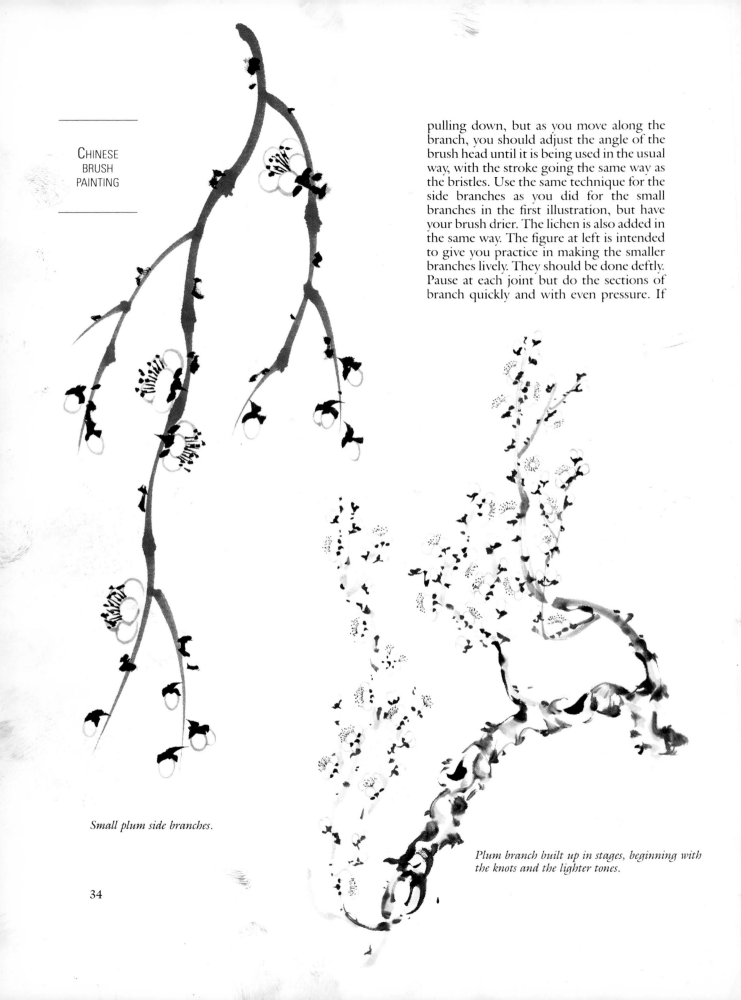

pulling down, but as you move along the branch, you should adjust the angle of the brush head until it is being used in the usual way, with the stroke going the same way as the bristles. Use the same technique for the side branches as you did for the small branches in the first illustration, but have your brush drier. The lichen is also added in the same way. The figure at left is intended to give you practice in making the smaller branches lively. They should be done deftly. Pause at each joint but do the sections of branch quickly and with even pressure. If

Small plum side branches.

Plum branch built up in stages, beginning with the knots and the lighter tones.

you are hesitant, your branch will look weak and unconvincing.

The last example (page 34) is built up gradually, starting with the knot holes, which are the focal points. To paint these, use a stroke similar to that used for the center sepal. After the knot holes, the light shading is done and, last, the darker outlining. Keep your brush lively and vary the pressure so that you impart texture and shape to your branch. The small branches are worked as in the previous three examples and so is the lichen.

Using color

Plum blossoms are usually painted in color, and shown below are various color schemes that can be used. For the outline flowers (**a**), first put a watery white wash over the petals. While this is still wet, blend yellow into the center of each flower. You can use ink for your stamens and pollen or you can do the stamens in vermilion and the pollen in thick yellow, vermilion, and red.

For the freestyle flowers (**b**), take a clean brush and dip it first into clear water. Wipe off the excess on the edge of the water jar and then just tip your brush into red. Paint the blossoms as you did when using ink. The effect of the water on the brush is to give two-tone petals since the color will bleed slightly into the clear portion of each stroke. Again, you can do the stamens in ink or in vermilion and the pollen in ink or in color. For a slightly different two-tone effect you can fill your brush with watery white instead of clear water before tipping it with red (**c**). Obviously if you want uniform-colored freestyle petals, you simply fill your brush with light color instead of ink. The sepals are always done in very black ink.

Freestyle branches do not have color applied to them, but the outlined ones can have a light brown wash. To achieve this, press down with the heel of the brush while gently moving the tip. Try to blend more than one shade on the branch.

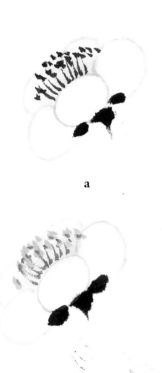

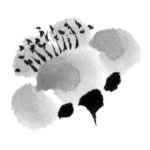

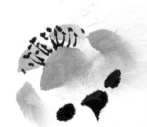

a

b

c

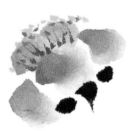

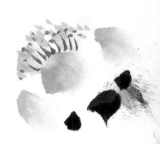

Colors for plum blossom flowers.

Common mistakes

The illustrations on this page show some of the mistakes commonly made by beginners. Below, in **a** the brush was not dried after mixing the ink and before being redipped to start the petal, so the ink has blurred too much; in **b** the stamens were not tapered by lifting the stroke off the paper into the air, and the sepals were drawn too deliberately; and in **c** the petal was drawn rather than formed by the brush being rolled; a white spot in the middle of the petal is the result. The illustration right shows what can happen when you are too hesitant with your branches and when you do not pause at the joints. The branch is thick and joined to the next one by a very flimsy thread.

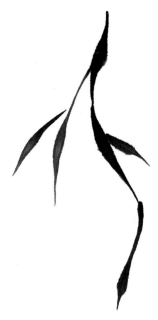

The joints of this plum blossom branch are stiff and unconvincing.

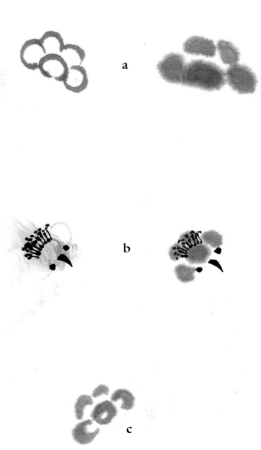

Some common mistakes in painting plum blossom flowers.

When you have practiced sufficiently to be confident of avoiding these errors and when you have executed a few lively and spirited plum blossom paintings of your own, try a more elaborate and complicated one like the painting shown opposite. After you have done a plum blossom painting that you like, turn to the chapter on washes (see page 115) and try your hand at a simple one. The painting on the right has a wash consisting of a combination of Assam tea and green tea. It was done on the back of the painting, which was laid on an old blanket and dampened before the wash was applied with light strokes, taking care to vary the direction of the brush and to create only subtle color variations.

Now that you are reasonably confident with plum blossoms, you are ready to go on to bamboo.

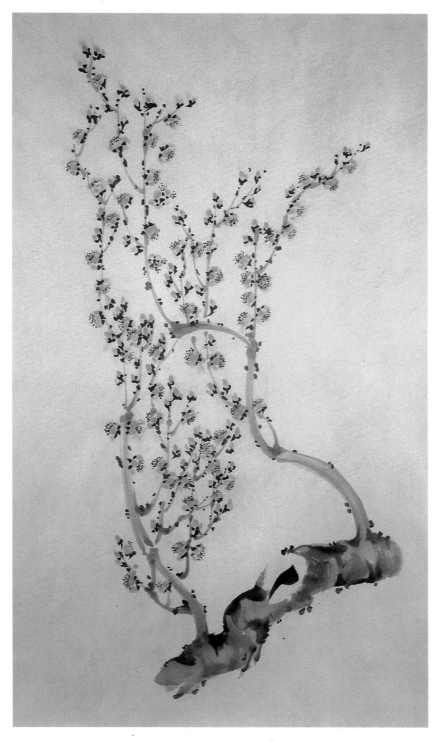

A finished plum blossom painting with a tea wash. The flowers are painted without using white, and the branch is given a simple brown wash before the tea is applied.

PAINTING BAMBOO

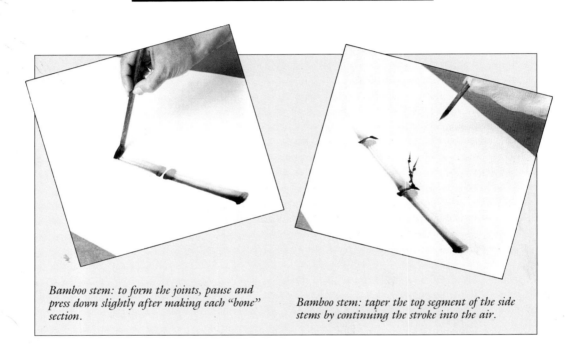

Bamboo stem: to form the joints, pause and press down slightly after making each "bone" section.

Bamboo stem: taper the top segment of the side stems by continuing the stroke into the air.

Bamboo is the gentleman of the Four Friends. The Chinese regard it as virtuous, hardy, upright, and gentle; it is also humble and consistent because it grows throughout all four seasons. The painting of bamboo is second only to landscape in prestige and is infinitely more important than the painting of animals or birds. A successful bamboo painting is almost the quintessence of Chinese painting.

You should try to visualize the whole before putting brush to paper and you must complete your rendering "in one breath," using the minimum of strokes and the maximum of élan. The ability to paint bamboo well is a reliable indicator that you will in time be able to master the techniques of Chinese brush painting.

Stems

Bamboo is greedy for ink, so you must begin by grinding plenty. You should also make an ample quantity of gray. Use a large brush and remember to rinse and dry it after mixing the gray.

To do a thick bamboo stem, as shown on page 39, in **a**, first saturate your brush with gray. Wipe off the excess moisture on the edge of your palette and tip the brush in black. Then, using the side of the brush, make your stem sections about 2½ to 3 inches long. Bamboo is always painted as it grows, from bottom to top. Pause slightly at the beginning and end of each stroke and move the brush quickly in the middle. This is known as the "bone" stroke. Leave a small space after each section and repeat the stroke again. Make the segments at the top slightly shorter than those at the base, and when you reach the top segment, taper it off by continuing the stroke into the air as you did for the ends of the plum branches. You must never redip your brush in mid-stalk; do not worry if the brush "misses" occasionally, as this will add texture. As you become more skilled, you can use a drier brush and create this effect deliberately (**b**). If you do not want the two-tone effect, you need not tip your brush with black before beginning.

For the narrower bamboo stem (**c**), take the same brush and again dip it in gray, wiping off the excess moisture. Holding the brush upright and again working from the bottom, make your segments in the "bone" manner, pausing slightly at the beginning and end of each stroke but moving fast in the middle. This time, however, your strokes are done in line with the bristles, not across them. Use the whole brush and make the segments longer than you did for the thicker stem. Remember to taper the top segment. The dark outline can be created by gently stroking the sides of your brush in black before starting the stem.

Stems can also be made without breaks, using the brush sideways (**d**) or lengthwise (**e**). Fill the brush and start as for the previous example, but instead of pausing at the

Bamboo stems.

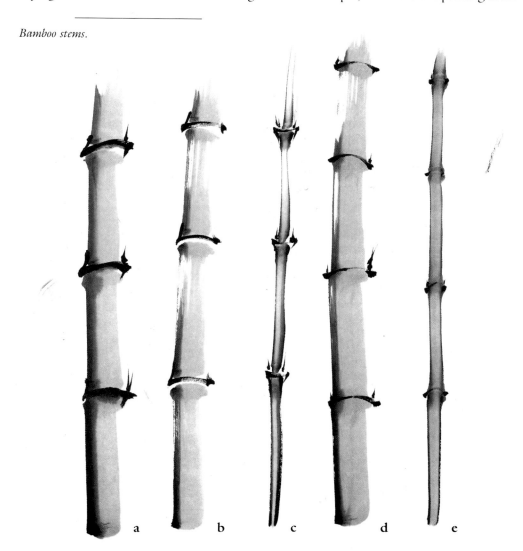

a   b   c   d   e

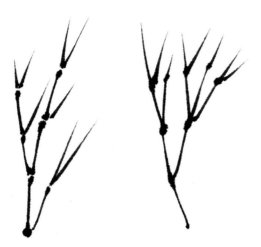

Small bamboo side stems.

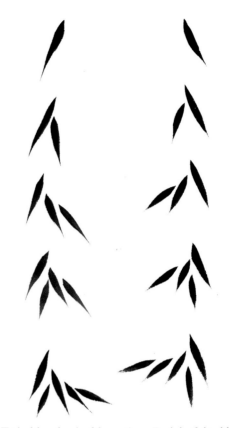

Typical bamboo leaf formations. Each leaf should be painted in one fluid movement.

end of each segment and lifting your brush, do a sideways squiggle while still working at the same speed. This will become the joint.

The illustration above shows the small side stems. These grow out of the joints and are painted with the tip of the brush. Usually they are done with short "bone" strokes and tapered final segments. Stems growing out of gapless bamboo (page 39, **d** and **e**) are done without lifting the brush between sections; to do these, pause and go back slightly instead.

The joints on the bamboo stem should be added while it is still wet, using very black ink. They are done fast, and although a variety of shapes is possible, you should be consistent within one picture.

Leaves

Bamboo leaves are not as easy to paint as they look. There is no substitute for plenty of practice. When first learning to do bamboo, you can fill enough rolls of paper to cover the walls of a sizable room with nothing but leaves.

First, saturate your brush with ink and wipe off the excess on the side of your palette. Hold the brush loosely about halfway up and keep it upright. Paint each leaf in one swift motion—down, along, up—starting and finishing the stroke in the air. Do not worry if the end splits; this is not serious if the leaf has form (it may even on

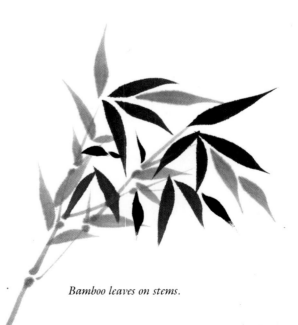

Bamboo leaves on stems.

occasion be the desired effect!). Bamboo leaves tend to get larger the farther they are from the base of the stem on which they are growing. Practice the formations on page 40, top right, and then try putting leaves on the stems (bottom right). Do the blackest leaves first and then the lighter ones; otherwise the black ink will run into the gray too much. The figure below shows how a complete bamboo stem is built up.

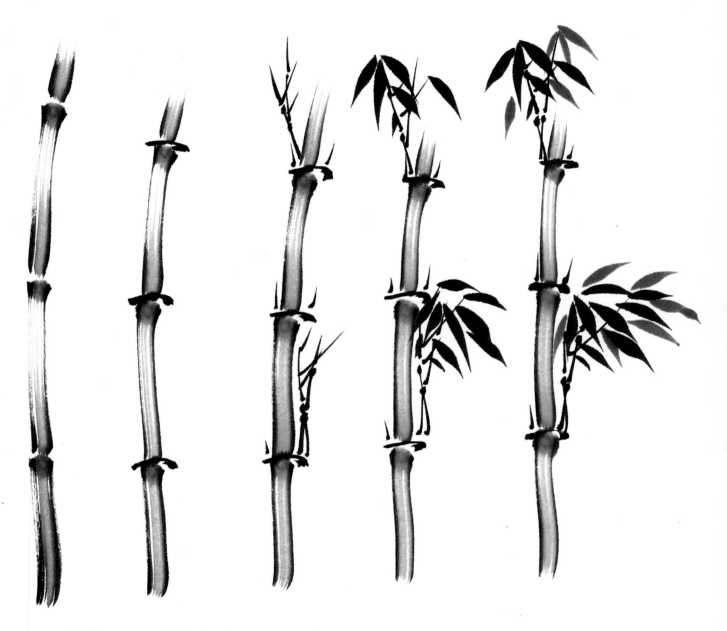

Building up a complete bamboo stem.

Common mistakes

While most students master bamboo stems fairly readily, a few typical errors do crop up. In the illustration below, for example, you can see that the joints in **a** are just arbitrary gaps because the brush pressure was too even; in **b** the brush was too wet and in **c** the brush was hesitant and the stem segments were made too long, the result being flat and unconvincing. Leaves usually cause problems at first for most beginners. The most common errors are the two shown at right. In **a** the stroke was carried on too long; and in **b** the movement of the branch was not fluid, resulting in a pause mid-leaf and a quick flick for the leaf tip.

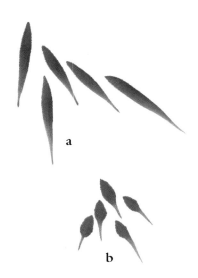

*Some common mistakes
in painting bamboo leaves.*

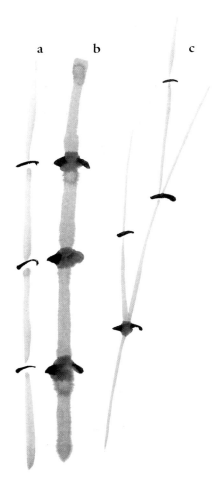

*Some common mistakes
in painting bamboo stems.*

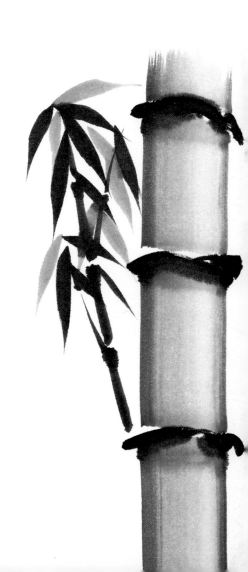

Fish made from bamboo leaf shapes.

You cannot practice bamboo leaves too much, but you may find the process slightly tedious after a while, so try putting the leaf shapes together to form other things, such as the fish illustrated above.

If you want to try some very dramatic bamboo, as shown below, use your wash brush. Soak the brush in light gray and then stroke the sides in black. The stem is then done in the same way as for **c** on page 39.

Obviously bamboo can also be done in color; the technique is exactly the same.

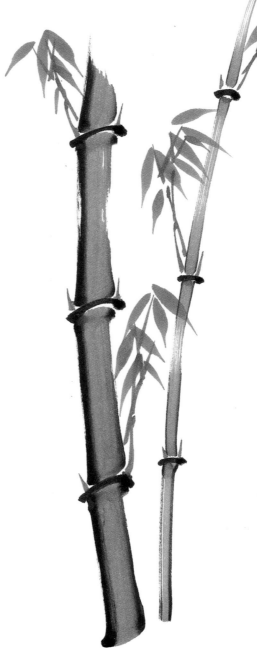

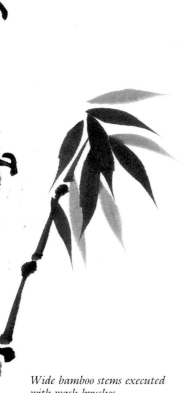

Wide bamboo stems executed with wash brushes.

Bamboo in color. Notice the use of space in the composition. The picture is very simple, yet it is satisfyingly complete.

PAINTING ORCHIDS

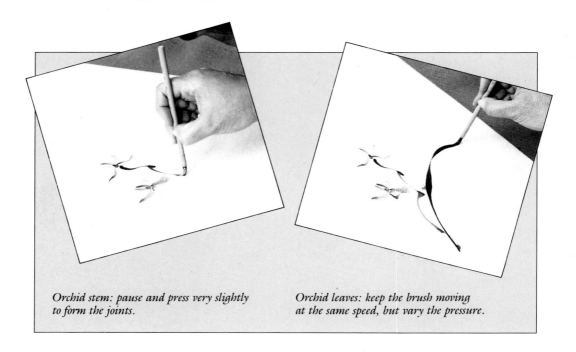

Orchid stem: pause and press very slightly to form the joints.

Orchid leaves: keep the brush moving at the same speed, but vary the pressure.

The orchid is believed by the Chinese to symbolize serenity in obscurity. Its perfume is highly prized, the more so because the flower tends to grow deep in inaccessible forests. It is essentially a feminine plant.

Flowers

Begin by painting the flowers. The figure at right indicates the order and direction in which you should paint the petals. First, dip your orchid brush in gray ink and wipe off the excess on the edge of your palette. Tip the brush in black ink. Start with the two central petals, **a** and **b**, pulling the brush in the direction of the arrows. You can always tell where the stroke was begun by the darker tone caused by the initial contact of the darkened brush tip with the

paper. Next do petal **c**, this time beginning from the center of the flower. Pull the brush outward with just the tip in contact with

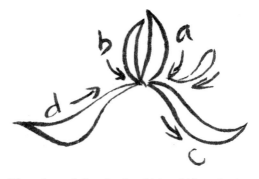

The order and direction in which orchid petals should be painted.

44

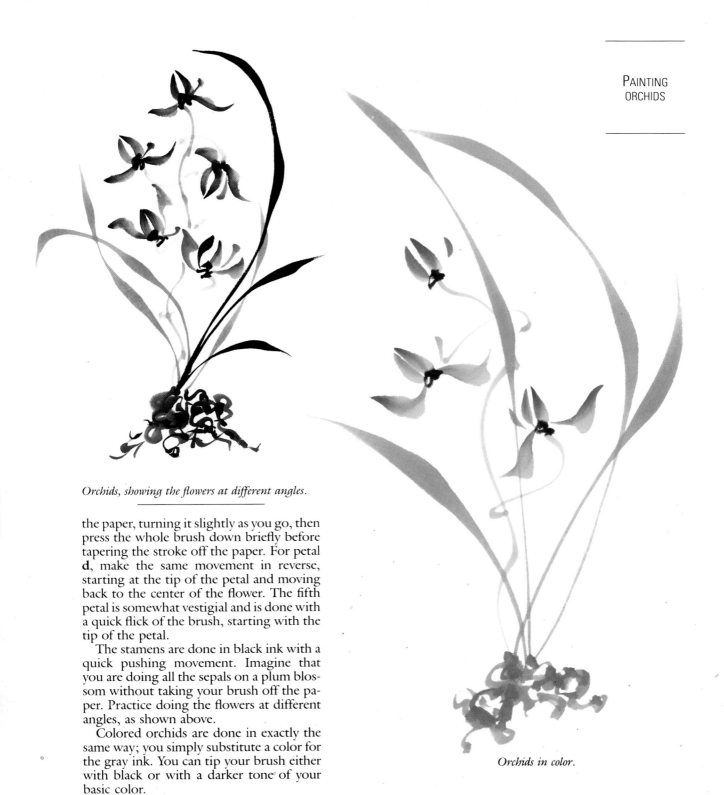

Orchids, showing the flowers at different angles.

the paper, turning it slightly as you go, then press the whole brush down briefly before tapering the stroke off the paper. For petal **d**, make the same movement in reverse, starting at the tip of the petal and moving back to the center of the flower. The fifth petal is somewhat vestigial and is done with a quick flick of the brush, starting with the tip of the petal.

The stamens are done in black ink with a quick pushing movement. Imagine that you are doing all the sepals on a plum blossom without taking your brush off the paper. Practice doing the flowers at different angles, as shown above.

Colored orchids are done in exactly the same way; you simply substitute a color for the gray ink. You can tip your brush either with black or with a darker tone of your basic color.

Orchids in color.

45

Stems

The stalk of the orchid must be done with speed and control, using light ink. As you did for the small plum branches, pause slightly to make the joints. The method for painting the orchid stem is an exception to the rule that things should always be painted in the direction they grow. You will find it much simpler to begin your stem at the top flower and work down toward the roots. Join the side flowers after you have done the main stem.

Leaves and roots

The leaves are done by varying the pressure of your brush. Load the brush fully with gray or black ink, depending on which leaf you are painting. Do the black ones first to avoid bleeding. Keep the brush moving at the same speed throughout the stroke, pressing down and lifting it as you go. Taper the end of each leaf. The roots are done with a twisting movement of the brush, using gray and black ink.

Common mistakes

More than almost any other subject in Chinese painting, orchids will come with sufficient practice. There are not many typical errors in orchid painting, but the illustration below shows a few that might arise. In **a** the brush was too dry; **b** shows the effect of holding the brush too stiffly; **c** was simply done too slowly; and **d** demonstrates what happens to the leaves if you are hesitant or turn the brush too much instead of varying the pressure.

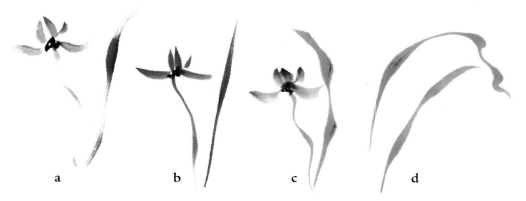

a   b   c   d

Some common mistakes in painting orchids.

PAINTING CHRYSANTHEMUMS

The chrysanthemum is highly valued because it is long-lasting and defies the frost by blooming in autumn. There are again two basic methods of painting it: outline and freestyle. As before, it is perfectly acceptable to combine the leaves of one method with the flowers of the other.

Flowers: outline method
For the flower in **a**, use a plum blossom brush and dip the tip in gray ink as you did for the outlined plum flowers. Mark the center of the flower and then draw the five petals that form the middle of the flower. Next, draw in the rest of the petals, slightly elongating them on one side of the flower and foreshortening them on the other. Take care always to have the petals growing in the right direction, that is, straight out from the flower center and not at an angle to it. When painting a side view (**b**), put in the sepals first and then draw the petals. The basic chrysanthemum design can have a variety of petal shapes (**c**), and a more elaborate outlined chrysanthemum is shown in **d**. The method for painting this is essentially the same. Remember, you should always strive for clear, fluid lines to your outline.

Flowers: freestyle method
The freestyle flowers shown at the top of page 48 are done with the brush fully loaded with gray ink, as for the freestyle plum blossom. Once again, put in the center of the flower first. Do the petals from the

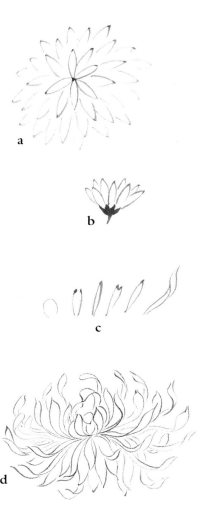

a

b

c

d

Outlined chrysanthemums.

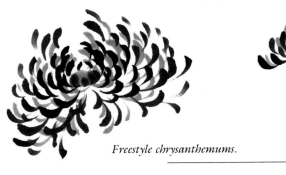

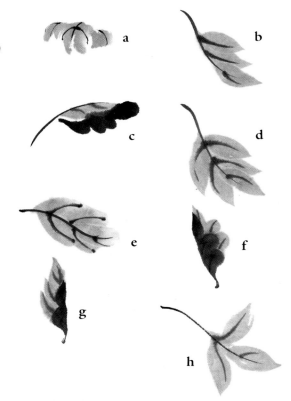

Freestyle chrysanthemums.

tip inward with a flicking movement like the one used for the fifth orchid petal. When you have done all the light petals, soak your brush in black and superimpose the darker petals. Extend the dark petals farther from the center than the light ones.

Leaves: outline method
The outlined leaves below should be fairly straightforward. Using only the tip of your brush, begin by putting in the center vein with a firm stroke tapered at the end. Then outline the leaf, using a thin but vigorous line.

Freestyle chrysanthemum leaves.

Leaves: freestyle method
The freestyle leaves shown above can be seen as a basic model for almost any kind of leaf. It is therefore important to practice them thoroughly so that you can tackle different leaves with confidence. Use a bamboo brush for all the leaves and always load it fully with ink. Remember to use the whole of your brush and not just the tip. Most of the fullness of a leaf is done by placing the heel of the brush on the paper and pressing, not by filling in the shape with strokes of the tip as a watercolorist would. For leaf **a**, do the central section first with a downward stroke of the side of the brush. Then add the two side sections with similar strokes, but only making contact with about half of the brush. Add the veins while the ink is still wet. In all the other examples here, the main vein is put in first, in black, with a tapering stroke. This gives you a reference point from which to build

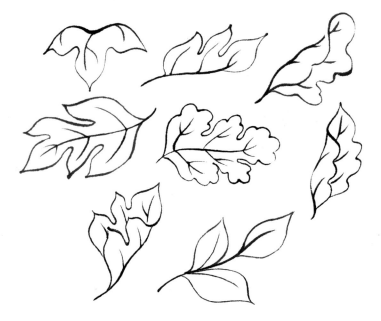

Outlined chrysanthemum leaves.

48

your leaf. Do not put in the subsidiary veins, however, as this will constrain you too much. For **b**, **d**, and **e**, put in the tip of the leaf first, then do the sections at the base, and last fill in the intervening ones. For **b**, **d**, and **h**, work from the outside in to create the points; begin by putting the tip of the brush on the paper and pull the stroke down toward the vein. As you pull, lay your brush fully on the paper and press down. One stroke should suffice for each leaf section. For **e**, the sections are done outward from the vein. Do the same move-ment as before but in reverse, using the heel of your brush not only to fill out the leaf but also to provide its rounded outline. For **c**, **f**, and **g**, do the rounded underside parts first, in the same way as plum petals. Finish the inside of the leaf with the method you used for **b**, **d**, and **h**. For **c**, do the inside of the leaf with a twisting movement, lifting and pressing the brush as you go. Try to add the side veins to your leaves before they have dried.

Stems
The stems of the chrysanthemums are done in the manner of plum blossom branches, but without any tapered sections.

Using color
Color is applied to the outlined flower be-low by using a single stroke for each petal.

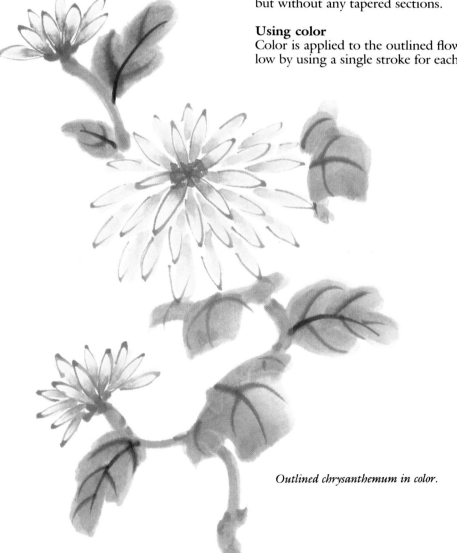

Outlined chrysanthemum in color.

49

Soak your brush in the basic color and wipe off any excess on the side of your palette. Tip the brush in a darker tone and then lay the brush on the petal with the tip toward its base. Push down the heel of your brush as you do this in order to fill in the outline. Do not worry if you do not manage to match your color exactly to the outline.

Notice that in this illustration freestyle leaves are used with an outlined flower. Usually these are done in gray first and then the color is added by repeating the same strokes on top of those already done, using a watery green wash. Remember, however, that the watery color should not be applied with a dripping wet brush. You must dry

your brush before dipping it in the green, as you do after mixing the gray ink. The water is needed as a constituent of the color rather than for its wetness.

Below left is the more elaborate kind of outlined chrysanthemum, and this time the color is blended on both the flowers and the leaves. The blending method is fully described in the section on painting a peony.

The freestyle flowers below right are simply achieved by substituting two different tones of the same color for the ink. The leaves are done as on page 49, but in this example no color wash was added. Obviously, you may color your leaves and stem if you wish.

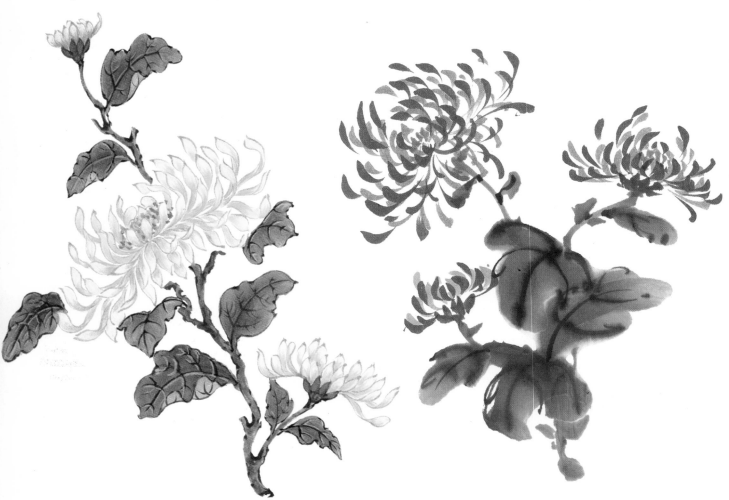

Detailed outlined chrysanthemums with blended color.

Freestyle chrysanthemums in color.

a

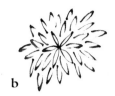

b

c

d

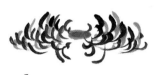

e

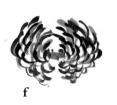

f

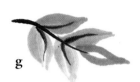

g

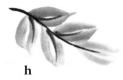

h

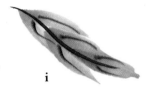

i

Some common mistakes in painting chrysanthemums.

Common mistakes

In addition to the usual mistakes caused by hesitancy, overworking, slowness, or misjudged quantities of ink, color, or water, which you should be able to recognize by now, there are a few errors that are peculiar to chrysanthemums and leaves. In the examples shown above, **a** is too small and cramped; **b** has petals growing in different directions, whereas they should always grow out from the center of the flower; **c** has too many layers (create the angle of viewing by lengthening or foreshortening the petals); **d** shows a freestyle flower that has lost its center and has stiff, lifeless petals; **e** looks as if it is growing in two clumps instead of being a rounded flower (take care to make your freestyle chrysanthemums fully rounded); **f** resembles a powder puff, extending too far vertically and not enough horizontally; the leaves in **g** were not painted with the whole of the brush (the brush was stroked like a Western brush and only the top was used, resulting in the need for too many strokes); in **h** the same mistake has also resulted in a marked tendency for the leaf segments to gap; and in **i** the segments were done in the wrong order, resulting in the leaf becoming elongated (always do the tip of the leaf first, then, leaving what looks like too small a space, paint the sections at the base and fill in the remaining sections); **i** also has side veins that look hesitant because they were not firmly joined to the spine.

PAINTING ROCKS

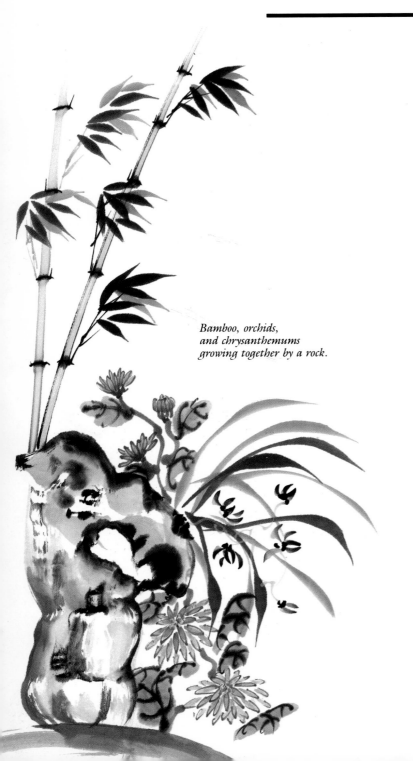

*Bamboo, orchids,
and chrysanthemums
growing together by a rock.*

Now that you have mastered all four of the Friends, you can try a composition that includes two or more of them. The example shown here uses a rock as an additional element, and since rocks feature frequently in Chinese paintings, it is useful at this stage to learn how to paint them.

In China the rock has come in a sense to symbolize the creative power of the earth itself. Westerners are sometimes bemused by the importance of rocks in Chinese art, so it is perhaps helpful for us to realize that the Chinese have used rocks in their gardens in the same way Europeans have used statuary. The contemplation of rocks is something that Chinese have long delighted in. Naturally, therefore, rocks have become an integral element of Chinese painting.

The examples on the right show the different styles of rocks often encountered in flower and bird paintings. They are worth mastering not only for their own sake but because you will later use essentially the same methods to paint rocks and mountains in landscapes. Think about rocks as you paint them; try to visualize the rock and feel its weight. This may sound pretentious, but it is surprisingly helpful. Always put in the gray shading first and then add the black.

In **a**, a wet brush was used for all the strokes, which were done with the tip of the brush. Figure **b** was also done with a wet brush, but this time the light shading and some of the black strokes were done with the side of the brush. Figure **c** was done with a dry brush and the texture was applied using the side of it. In **d**, the wash was blended to form the shape of the rock and then the black was applied while the wash was still wet. Remember always to use as large a brush as you can manage.

Rocks can also have a color wash, or you can use a thicker blending of color applied in the manner described for Lingnam lotus leaves (see page 71).

Rocks do not seem to produce any problems that are peculiar to themselves. Remember, as always, to try to visualize the finished shape before putting brush to paper. Also, try to apply each stroke with spontaneity and dash, and do not use more than are necessary.

c

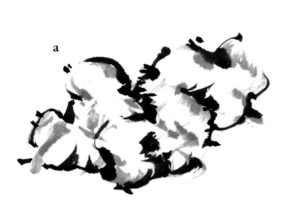

a

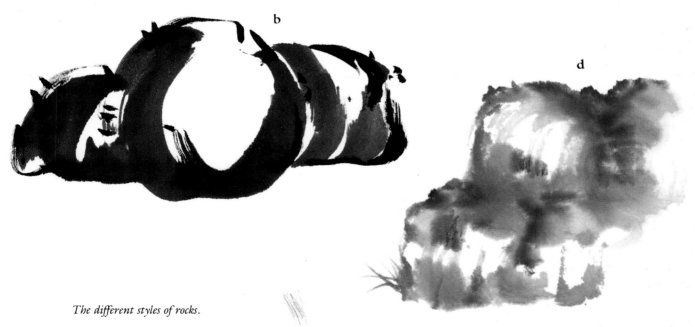

b

d

The different styles of rocks.

PAINTING PINES

The pine tree is a symbol of longevity and is often depicted with cranes, which are particularly long-lived birds. The pine also stands for the constancy of friendship in adversity. It is thought of as the king of trees, and this is presumably why, unlike other tree species, it has come to be studied on its own in Chinese painting courses and manuals.

There is no real difference between painting pines freestyle and outline, although you should use a larger brush for freestyle and make fewer strokes.

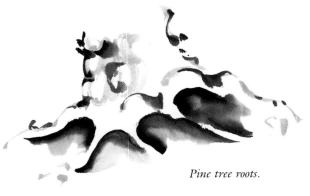

Pine tree roots.

Trunk, branches, and roots

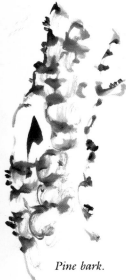

Pine bark.

Begin by practicing the bark as shown left. If a branch or tree trunk has a knot in it, you should do this first, as you did when doing plum branches. Then, using a large dry brush and gray ink, do the shading by making rough circular shapes with the side of your brush. Do not make the circles too uniform and only paint enough to cover about half of the width of your branch or tree trunk. Use some semicircles toward the center of the trunk. Still using gray ink, draw in the side of the branch or trunk that you have not shaded, using strokes similar

to those for outlining the plum branch on page 34. Then, apply the black strokes, using the tip of your brush. While applying these strokes, vary the pressure of your brush on the paper.

The side branches shown below are done like the freestyle plum branches at the top of page 33 but with even more panache so that they give the impression of being flung onto the paper. Give them an upward sweep.

For the tree roots shown above, fill your brush with gray ink and then dip it in black

Pine side branches.

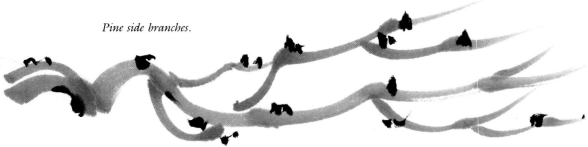

to about halfway up the bristles. Paint the hollows of the roots with a twisting motion similar to that used for a large knot hole. Put in the root outlines with gray and black.

Needles and cones

There are many species of pine trees, and each has its own configuration of needles, but **a**, below, shows the form of pine needles most usually depicted in Chinese brush painting. Once you have mastered their execution, you can adapt the shape to suit your own needs. You may find it helpful at first to put in an inverted T shape and fill in the needles around it. While **a** has tapered needles, **b** has blunt ones and fewer of them, which creates a more freestyle effect. Pine needles tend to grow upward from a branch, but try to vary the angle slightly and overlap your groups of needles.

The pine cones shown below are done in black with a flicking movement of the brush tip. Begin at the top of the cone and work back toward the base. The closer together you put the strokes, the more closed the cone will look. In a painting, when a pine tree forms part of a landscape and is intended to be seen from a distance, the cones are often shown by means of black spots.

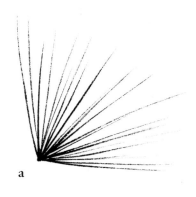

a

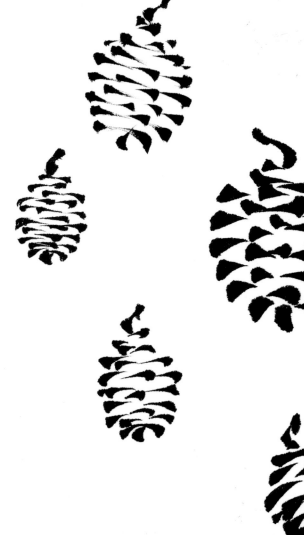

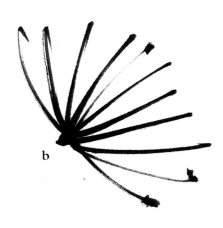

b

Pine needles.

Pine cones.

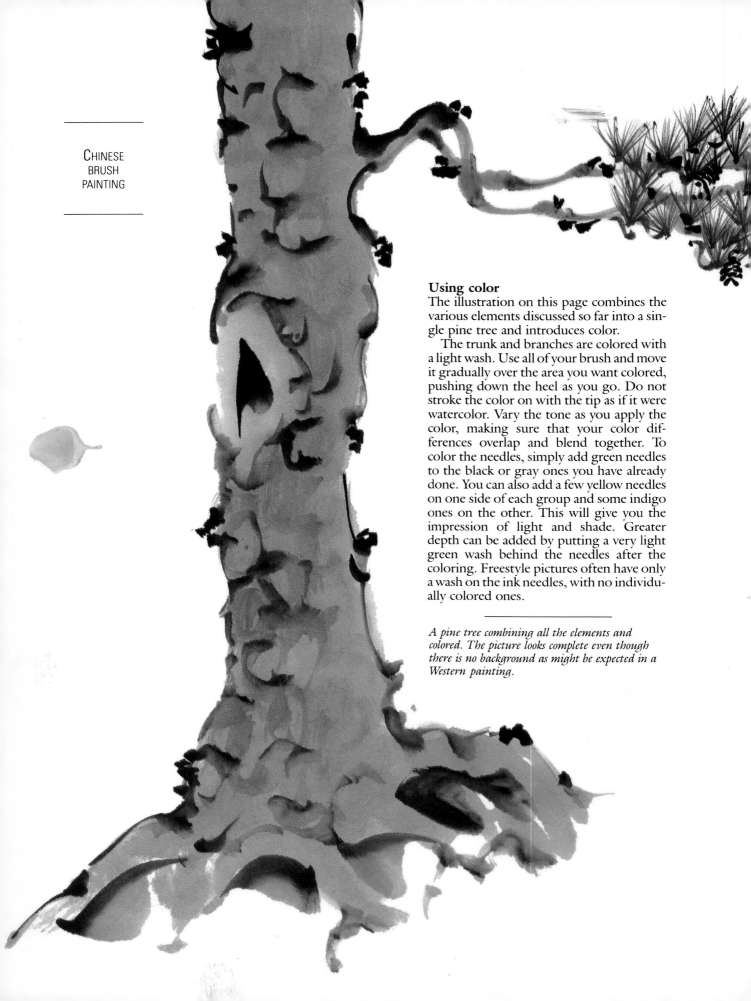

Using color

The illustration on this page combines the various elements discussed so far into a single pine tree and introduces color.

The trunk and branches are colored with a light wash. Use all of your brush and move it gradually over the area you want colored, pushing down the heel as you go. Do not stroke the color on with the tip as if it were watercolor. Vary the tone as you apply the color, making sure that your color differences overlap and blend together. To color the needles, simply add green needles to the black or gray ones you have already done. You can also add a few yellow needles on one side of each group and some indigo ones on the other. This will give you the impression of light and shade. Greater depth can be added by putting a very light green wash behind the needles after the coloring. Freestyle pictures often have only a wash on the ink needles, with no individually colored ones.

A pine tree combining all the elements and colored. The picture looks complete even though there is no background as might be expected in a Western painting.

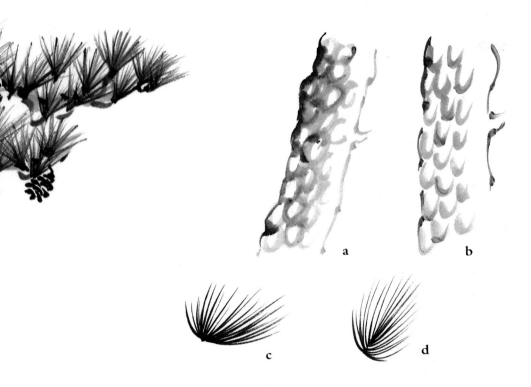

Some common mistakes in painting pines.

Common mistakes

Pictured above are the most common mistakes beginners make with pines. In **a** the brush was not dry enough for the shading and the circles are too neat; the brush tip was used instead of the side; in **b** there are too many semicircles and insufficient completed ones; avoid the temptation to do little scooping strokes; in **c** the needle group is unbalanced and the individual nee- dles are too curved; and in **d** the center point of the needle group has drifted. Other errors that can mar a painting of a pine tree occur in the coloring. Often the trunk looks blotchy because too little care was taken to blend the wash, and students occasionally get carried away and make the needles rather garish by adding too much yellow and indigo. Sometimes they forget to put the green needles in at all.

57

PAINTING GRASSES

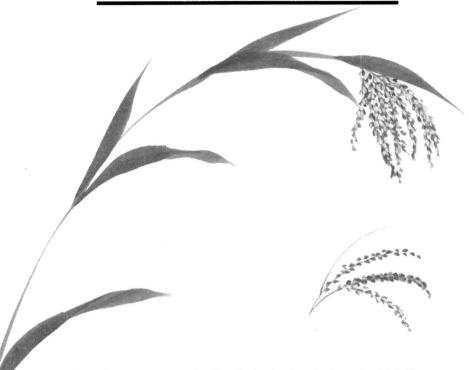

Flowering grass stem in color. Detail, showing how the flower head is built up.

The Mustard Seed Garden Manual of Painting has a section entitled "Book of Grasses and Insects," but closer examination reveals that it is concerned mainly with such flowers as orchids, chrysanthemums, and peonies. Only four pages are devoted to grasses as we think of them, and even these are concerned with grasses simply as ground cover in landscapes and flower paintings. Grass is seldom the main feature of a Chinese painting, but it is used so often to enhance pictures of flowers, birds, and insects that it merits a section of its own here.

The normal distinction between outline and freestyle methods does not have much relevance to painting grass since it is very seldom outlined. The chief difference between the grass in a *gongbi* painting and that in a *xieyi* one is that the former is more painstakingly and tidily executed. If you want to try outlining grass, draw it with a fine-pointed brush.

Flowering grass stem
The illustration above shows a flowering grass stem in color. To paint this, do the stalk first, using a yellowish green. Imagine

you are painting a thin, curved bamboo stem and you will achieve the correct effect (bamboo is, after all, a grass). Likewise, the leaves are done in much the same way as bamboo leaves, although they should be slightly longer and some of them should be turned by varying the brush pressure in the same way as for orchid leaves (see page 46). Use a slightly bluer green for these. For the flower head, first draw in the stems with the point of your brush. Make the seeds by pressing slightly with the tip of the brush, starting with gray seeds and adding purple or yellow ones. As a final touch you can add some white seeds, remembering that the more white you add, the riper your grass will look.

Other grasses

The grass below is done with a "feather" or "split-brush" stoke. Do not have your brush too dry or you will not achieve an even stroke. *Split* does not necessarily imply *dry*. First do the stem rather like a thin orchid leaf (see page 46), using only the tip of your brush. Then splay out the bristles and add the feathery fronds by working outward from the stem.

At right are a few examples of the grass and undergrowth often used in the foreground of landscapes.

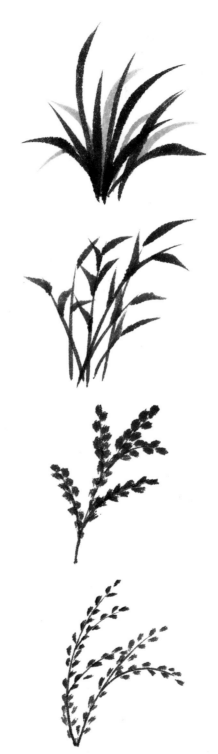

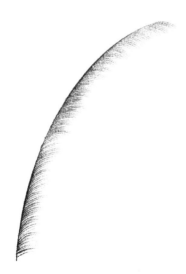

"Feathered" grass stem.

Grass and undergrowth frequently used in the foreground of landscapes.

59

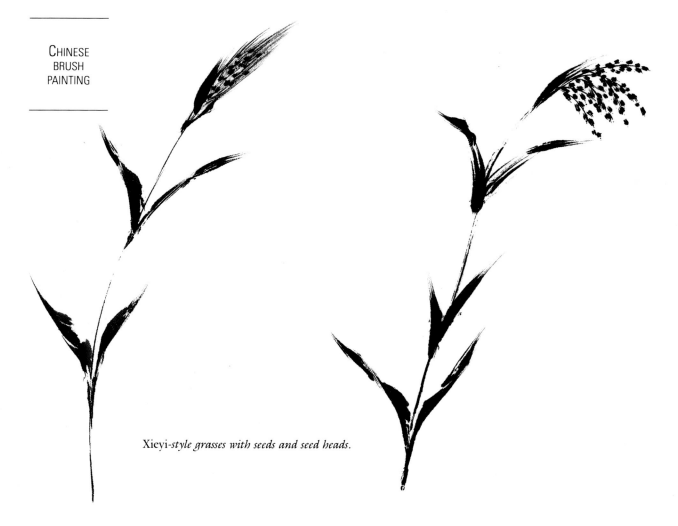

Xieyi-*style grasses with seeds and seed heads.*

Xieyi-style grasses

The figure above illustrates some freestyle grasses of the type that frequently occur in *xieyi* paintings of birds and animals. Ideally they should be done with a horsehair brush (see page 22) but it is possible to do them with a dry wolf-hair brush with its tip twisted so that the end splays out slightly to give a split effect. Instead of pulling the brush to form the stem as you did for the flowering grass stem (page 58), reverse the stroke and push the brush to make the stem

segments. The leaves are done in the same way as before but the effect of the horsehair brush is to make them look unkempt. The grass heads are also done with a horsehair brush. Of course, these *xieyi* grasses can also be done in color.

Common mistakes

Grass does not usually present many problems for the beginner, although some people have a tendency to be too neat, especially with freestyle examples.

PAINTING THE PEONY

There are a number of flower species for which the methodology is essentially the same. Of these, the one most commonly depicted in Chinese painting is the peony, which is known to the Chinese as "the king of flowers" and the "flower of nobility and wealth."

Flowers: outline method

For the outlined flower below, left, begin by deciding where the center of your flower is and marking it in lightly. For the half-open flower, lightly outline the sepals in green before you put in the petals. For both examples, outline the petals, working from the center of the flower outward and using a darker tone of the color you are going to paint them. It is crucial to have a clean, firm, expressive line.

There are two ways of coloring the petals. The first, as shown in **a**, is by blending. Always blend from light to dark. Fill the petal with the lightest shade, or with white

if you want a very pale flower; without rinsing your brush, tip it in a darker shade; place the brush so that the tip comes where you want the darkest tone to be (usually the base of the petal or around the edge) and press down, running the darker color over the light one; rinse and dry the brush and blend the tones together with a clean brush. If your color is not dark enough, you can add more and reblend, but be careful not to overwork and make the paint too thick or scuff the paper.

Always finish one petal before going on to the next. You can save time by applying all the light color first and then going around again with the darker shade, but the effect will be somewhat striped because the light tones will dry before you can add the dark ones. Relax and take your time; color blending is a soothing occupation. Try to keep the color from running outside the petal shapes, but do not worry too much if it does. Simply wash over the edges of the

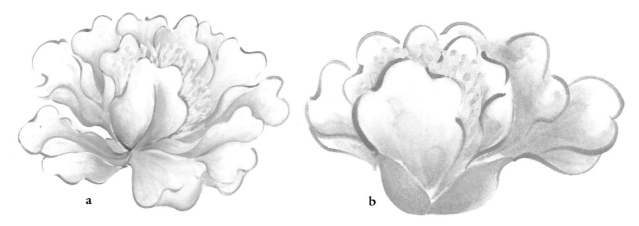

a   b

Outlined peony flowers.

run with clean water to prevent a water-mark (this may make it run further but do not panic), and when you later put a wash on your painting, use a tone that will blend with the color so that you finish up with a darker-toned halo to your flower. You may also be able to avoid the problem of color running to some extent by adding more white to your darker tones.

The second method of coloring peonies is illustrated in **b** on page 61. It gives a more delicate effect but is not suitable if you plan to add a wash to your picture, because the petals will pick up the background color. Fill your brush with water and put just the tip in some fairly diluted color. Then place the tip of your brush at the base of the petal and press down with the heel of the brush, trying to fill the petal with one movement.

It is not practical to use this method for flowers that are darker at the edges since it is almost impossible to prevent the wetness from flooding over the edges. This does not matter, however, if your color is concentrated in the center of the flower because it will only be water that runs outside the outline.

Whichever method of coloring you use, you should add the stamens in white or yellow.

Flowers: freestyle method
For the freestyle peony below, take a large brush (bamboo size or bigger) and saturate it with the lightest shade. Next, dip the brush about halfway up the bristles into a darker shade, then dip the very end of the brush into still darker color. Decide where

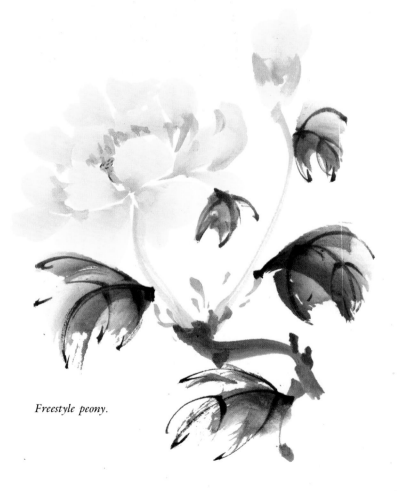

Freestyle peony.

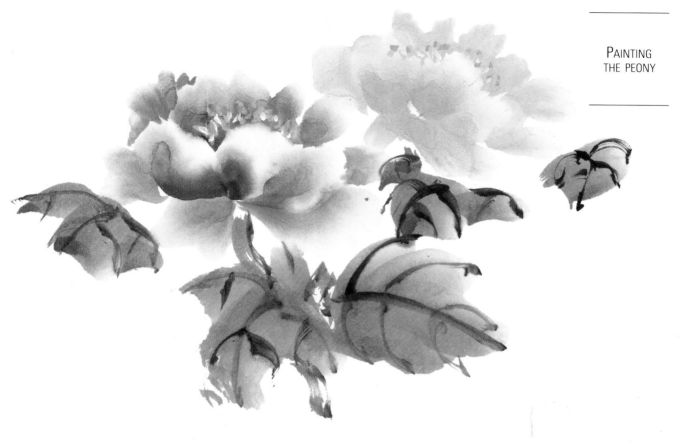

Freestyle peony with water substituted for the lightest tone.

the center of your flower is and place the tip of your brush at this point. Press down the heel of the brush, moving the base sideways while keeping the tip still, then lift the brush cleanly off the paper. Do the other petals in the same way, remembering that you will not be able to see the bases of all the petals and adjusting the colors on your brush accordingly. Add the stamens with thick gouache white and tip them in yellow, orange, and red at random. For the side view, remember to put the sepals in before the petals, as with the outline peony. Sometimes it is permissible to blend in a little color on the edges of the petals as well, to give your flower more shape.

If you want to reverse the color sequence of your petals by having the darkest tones on the outer edges, you can do this in two ways. You can either fill your brush with a light color, very carefully dipping just the heel into a darker color, and then use the same method as before, or you can load the brush as previously described but reverse the technique. This means that you should place the brush on the paper with the heel toward the middle of the flower, then swing the darkened tip of the brush around to form the outside edge of the petal.

The two-tone effect in freestyle flowers can also be achieved without using two or three colors. Wash your brush in clear water and dip about half the bristles into a diluted color. Tip the end of the brush in concentrated color and use the brush as you did before, pressing down the heel and moving it gently sideways. An example of this method is shown above.

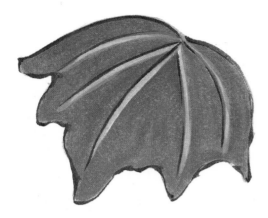

Outlined peony leaf with the color applied by blending.

Leaves: outline method

The outlined leaf shown above is done by first drawing the veins in very light green and then lightly marking in the outline. The color is applied by blending in the same way as for petals, starting by bringing a brownish tone in from the outer edges and running fresher green out from the center. Use a dry brush and make your color mixture quite rich so that you can leave the veins with an unpainted line alongside them. If your color runs so that you lose the white veins, or if you prefer not to try to leave a space for them, you can draw them on when the color is dry, using opaque light green. Outline the leaf with very dark green or brown, using a lively line with varied pressure, and enhance the veins by putting in a dark line on one side of the white or green vein (following your original faint line). This time use a smooth stroke tapering at the tip. Vary the shape and style of your leaves depending on the species of flower you are painting.

Leaves: freestyle method

The freestyle leaves are done in the same way as the chrysanthemum leaves on page 48, taking account of their different shapes. In other words, put in the center vein and build the leaf around it by doing the top section first, followed by the base sections. Fill in the intermediate segments and the side veins last. Use a large soft brush for the leaves.

Other flowers

After you have practiced a few peonies, try a magnolia (below), using the outline method; the technique is essentially the same. Do the stems and leaves freestyle first

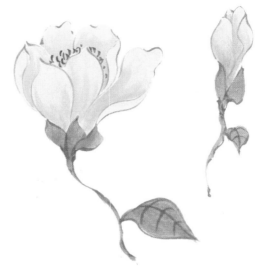

Magnolia in the outlined and blended method.

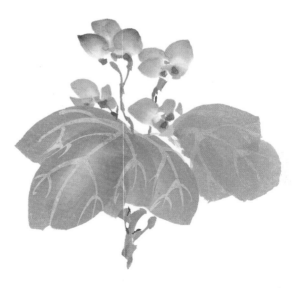

Usually flowers are painted before leaves, but in this case, the begonia leaves should be done first because they dominate the picture. The veins are drawn in white before the color is added to the leaves. Again the composition is very simple.

and then outline them. Similarly, try some of the other freestyle flowers illustrated here. Once you have mastered the technique of painting peonies, there is no reason why you should not attempt any kind of flower you wish to paint in either the outline or the freestyle method.

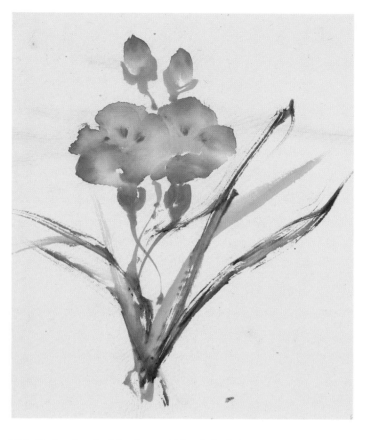

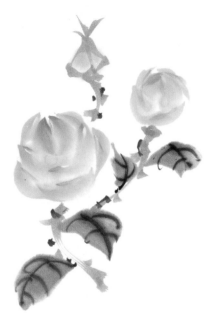

The method for painting this rose is similar to that of the freestyle peony, but highlights are added with strokes of color and white while the petals are wet. The bud should be outlined before the color is filled in.

This lily is painted with a large soft brush loaded with water and tipped with diluted color. The petals are painted in much the same way as plum blossom petals, although on a larger scale, and then the funnel-shaped flower bases, stalks, and leaves are added.

Common mistakes

The most common errors made in *gongbi* flower paintings are inadequate blending and poor shape. Always blend carefully and do not dilute the color too much or it will flood out of your petals. This will also happen if you forget to blend from light to dark. The effect of adding white to a water-based color is to cause the color to run out. In any case, your color will not blend properly unless you work from light to dark. Do not make your white too thick or your flowers will look heavy. To achieve good shape, keep the whole flower in mind as you draw each petal so that you maintain a balance. Make your outline strokes clean and lively.

For the freestyle flowers, load your brush carefully and remember to use as few strokes as possible, making each one count. Use your whole brush. Mistakes that crop up regularly are usually the result of overworking with too little of the brush or of too diluted color. The leaves present problems similar to those described in the section on chrysanthemums (see page 51).

PAINTING THE LOTUS

Although it is another large-petaled flower, the lotus merits a section of its own. It is an important theme in Chinese painting and its leaves are unlike any we have dealt with so far. In addition, there is a way of painting lotus, originated by the Lingnam school, that is quite different from anything you have tackled before, while being firmly rooted in the traditions of brush painting.

The lotus is a symbol of summer and fruitfulness. It represents purity and perfection. The flowers are normally either white or pink, and the leaves are dark bluish-green on top and light green underneath. The edges of the leaves start to turn brown almost as soon as they reach full size.

Gongbi-style lotus

The outlined lotus flower shown opposite is done in the same way as the peony (see page 61). Lightly outline the seed pod and then draw in the petals using a fine-pointed brush. For colored flowers it is effective to outline the petals in red and then blend the colors as you did before. Run a weak yellow wash over the inner surfaces of the petals after you have blended the pink. These inner surfaces should be very pale; the outer surfaces can be quite deep pink. You can add fine veins to the petals by using a feather stroke and red paint. Blend light and dark green for the seed pod, adding a tinge of red to your brush tip. Put in the black seed holes with gouache yellow centers. If you have no gouache yellow, mix Chinese or Japanese yellow with gouache white to achieve the desired opacity. The stamens are also done in opaque yellow and the pollen in yellow, orange, and red.

Draw the leaves in very light green. You will probably find it easiest to achieve a pleasing shape if you first mark in the center and the veins lightly and then work the outline around these. Note that some lotus veins are forked at the end and some are not. When you have established the shape, dampen the leaf all over with clean water. Shade the darker areas of the upper side of the leaf with ink, taking care to blend from nearly black to almost clear without sudden changes of density. Apply the ink as you did the wash to the plum blossom branch, by pressing down with the heel of your brush while gently moving the tip. When the paper has dried, add the color to the leaf, blending it as you work. Use fairly thick color and once again move the brush very gradually over the leaf area, pressing down with the heel as you go. Blend in brown, orange, yellow, and even some white at the edge and around any holes you have in your leaf. Before the color is quite dry, outline the leaf again in greenish black, using an uneven pressure on the point of the brush. Add the veins and the center last, using very light green mixed with gouache white to make it opaque. Pick out one side of each vein with the color you used for outlining the leaf. The underside of a lotus leaf has no ink shading, but the color is blended in the same way as on the upper side. Use a light yellowish-green as your predominant color. The veins on the underside should be darker than those on the upper leaf surface.

The stalks of the leaves and the flowers are the same. Using a plum blossom brush, fill the bristles with brownish-green and dip the sides in a dark reddish tone as you might

Gongbi *lotus, using blended color for the flowers. An ink wash is applied on the top of the leaves before the color is blended in.*

66

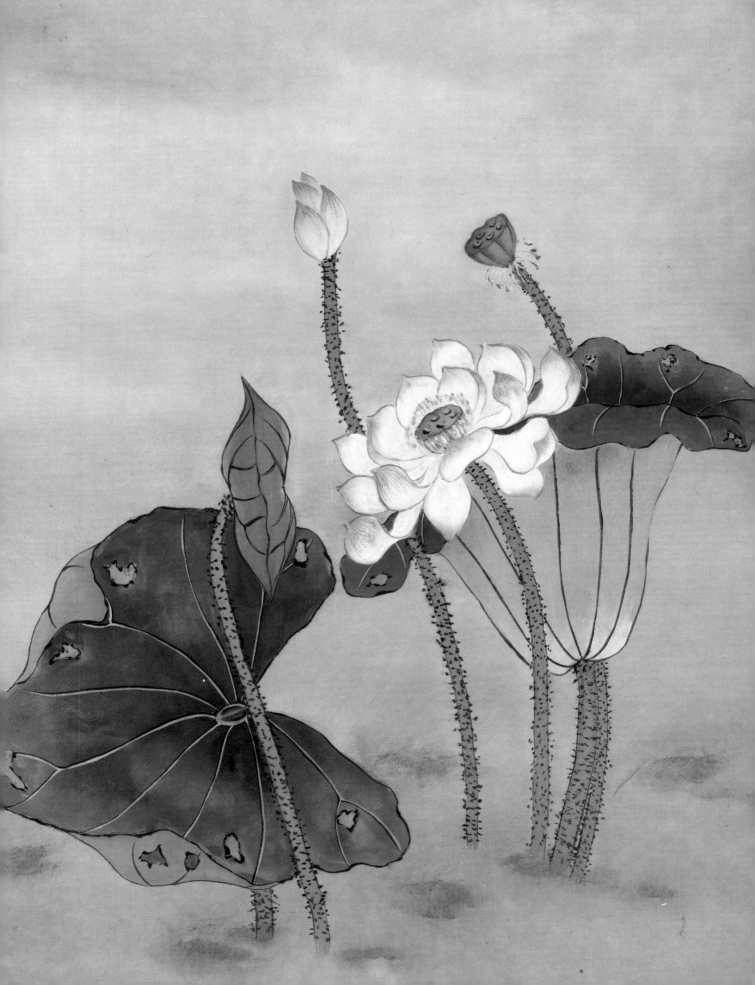

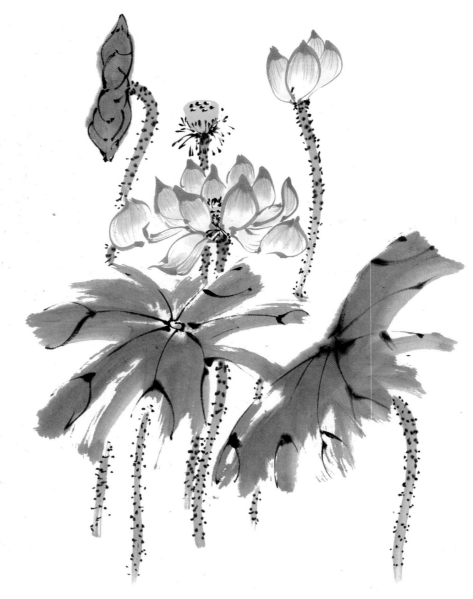

for a bamboo stem. Begin painting the stalk at the flower or leaf and work downward. Add the black dots for the hairs on the stalk immediately before it has time to dry. To learn how to complete your picture, turn to the wash section on page 115.

Xieyi-style lotus

The flower illustrated below is also outlined, but in the *xieyi* style. Use a horsehair brush to make vigorous strokes in gray, black, or red. Often this style of flower is found in an ink painting, but if you want to add color to the petals, you should use diluted color, as described in the section on peonies (see page 62). However, there is a slight difference in technique because you have two focuses of color—pink at the top of the petal and yellow at its base.

Fill a large brush with water and dip the

Xieyi *lotus with outlined flowers.*

68

end in diluted red. Place the brush inside the petal outline with the tip toward the top edge. Press down the heel of the brush to spread the water. Then wash your brush and tip it in very diluted yellow. Repeat the process, this time placing the tip of your brush at the base of the petal and making sure that when you press down with the heel of the brush, the moisture spreads into that left by the earlier stroke. The stamens are done in black, yellow, or red, depending on the general color scheme of your picture, and the pollen should be the same color as the stamens.

The leaves are usually done in gray with black veins even if the flower is outlined in red. Use a very large brush, preferably a soft white one and soak it with dark gray ink. Work the shape of the leaf from the inside outward, using as few strokes as possible and pressing down the heel firmly to make the outside edge of the leaf. While the leaf is still wet, add the veins, using a dry brush and very black ink. Remember to vary the forked veins with the unforked ones. The stalks are also done in gray with black splotches.

At right is a *xieyi* lotus done by the non-outline method. The center of the flower, the seed pod, is painted with a single pressed-down stroke, using a large brush loaded with yellow. The black seed holes are added on top. The petals are done like free-style peony petals, but remember that lotus petals tend to be darker at the top, so this is where you should place the tip of your brush, pressing down the heel to make the lighter base of the petal. Use a clean brush loaded with water and tipped in red for a translucent effect, but for a more substantial flower, load your brush in pink or yellow made with white paint and tip in red. The stamens should be white with yellow pollen or yellow with orange and red pollen, or you can do them in black, as shown here.

The leaves and stalk are done in the same way as for the illustration left, but you can add a green wash on top.

Lingnam-style lotus

The painting shown on page 70 is done quite differently from the previous three examples, and the wash is an integral part of

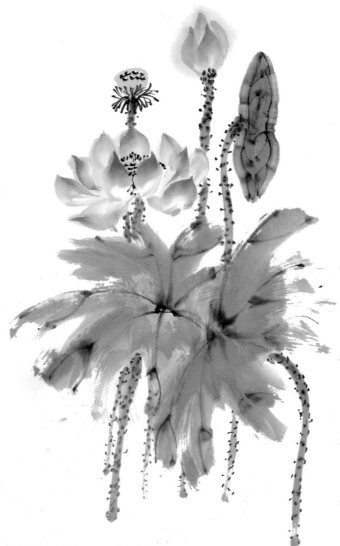

Xieyi lotus with nonoutlined flowers.

the picture. The other lotus styles can be enhanced by a wash, but in this case the wash is essential and you will therefore need to consult page 115. You will find it a little simpler if you sketch the outline of the leaves lightly in charcoal. It is a a feature of this method that everything runs, and if you mark your leaf edges in ink, they will probably finish in the wrong place. Rub off the excess charcoal and shade the leaves as you did for the *gongbi* lotus (page 66). This time, however, the color is added on top of the ink shading while the ink is still wet.

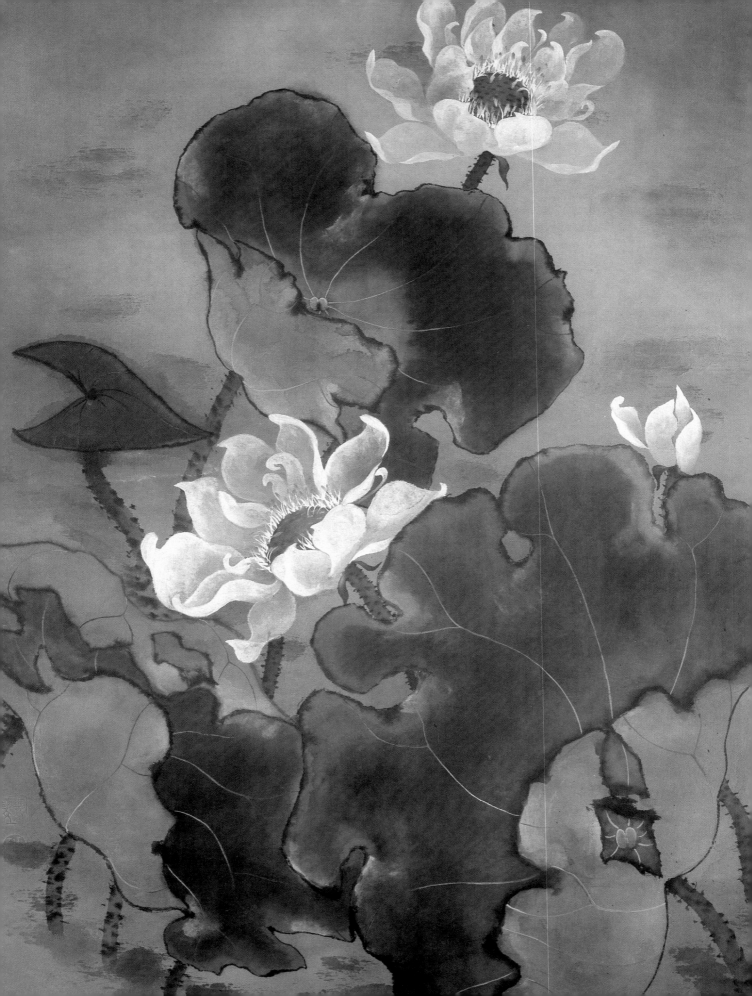

Blend the color in the same way and do not worry if it spreads because of the wetness of the paper. Make the edges of the leaves and around the holes nicely irregular with plenty of brown, orange, yellow, and white blended in. As before, the undersides have no ink shading and are predominantly light green. Allow the leaves to dry partially. When they are just damp and have completely stopped spreading, add the outline of the leaf using a horsehair or twisted wolf-hair brush and black ink, remembering to leave spaces in the outline where your flowers are going to be. Last, add the veins as you did for the leaves on page 66.

The stalks, which are the same as those on page 68 but are done in color, should be painted next. Make sure you put in stalks for the flowers even though you have not done these yet.

Allow the painting to dry and then add a wash, blending blues, greens, and browns as described in the section on washes. Use a fair amount of color so that the places where your leaf color has spread blends into the background. When the wash is almost dry, add a few lily pads by filling a large soft brush with dark green tipped with brown and pressing down sideways on the paper.

After the wash has completely dried, you can add the flowers. This is one of the very few occasions when you add anything to a picture after the wash is done. Put in the flower center (the seed pod), using a large brush loaded with bluish-green and tipped with dark red. Load a large soft brush with very diluted gouache white and tip it in concentrated white. Then do the petals as you would normally for a freestyle flower. Remember, when deciding on the thickness of your paint, that white is more opaque when dry than wet. Add a few dense white small petals around the seed pod and some thick white undersides of petals and turned-in edges. Run a very thin yellow wash over the inner surfaces of the petals. Make sure each flower joins the stalk you have painted for it. Finally do the stamens in very thick white and the pollen in yellow, orange, and red, then add the sepals.

Common mistakes

Lotus flowers present much the same sort of problems as peonies and other large-petaled flowers. Take particular care when painting white flowers to get the correct variation in the density of white. The most common mistake with all styles of the lotus leaf is patchy color. To avoid this, take time when blending and press down firmly with the heel of your brush while moving it very gradually over the leaf area.

The Lotus Pond. *Painted in the Lingnam style, this picture is an example of one of the few instances when anything is added to a painting after the wash has been done—in this case, the white flowers (private collection).*

$\mathcal{P}$AINTING INSECTS

With the possible exception of horses and birds, the Chinese have traditionally placed a low value on paintings of fauna. They have considered flora, particularly bamboo, and above all landscapes to be more worthwhile subjects for artists. Indeed, *The Mustard Seed Garden Manual of Painting* relegates insects to the last few pages of its "Book of Grasses and Insects," and heads each of these pages with the words "Examples of insects for paintings of grasses and herbaceous plants." In other words, the plant is intended to be the main subject—the insect merely an enhancement. Japanese painters have, on the whole, paid more attention to insects and have given them a more prominent place in compositions. The Lingnam school, however, has fully exploited the potential of insects.

Outline method
The illustrations below and at the top of page 73 show outline-method insects, the kind used in pictures of large-petaled

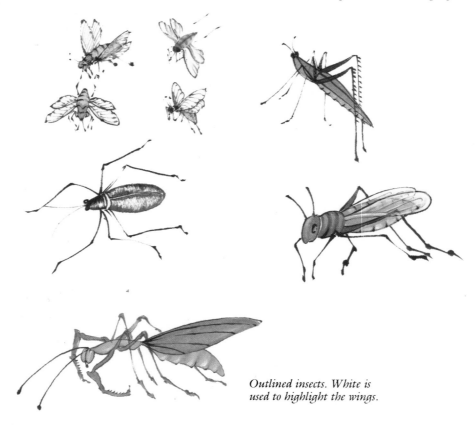

Outlined insects. White is used to highlight the wings.

72

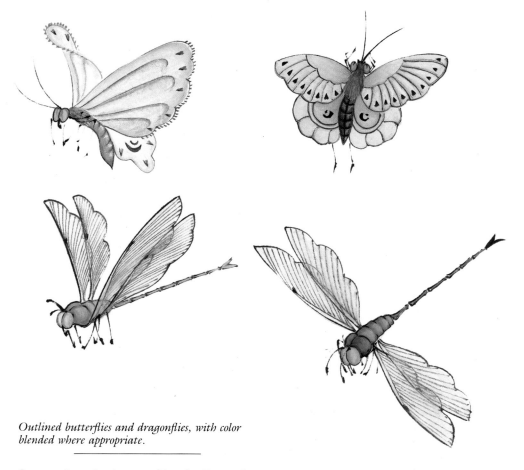

Outlined butterflies and dragonflies, with color blended where appropriate.

flowers done in the *gongbi* style. Draw the outlines with a fine-pointed brush and then fill in the shapes, using colors found in nature or whichever you like. Blend where it is appropriate to do so—for example, on butterfly wings. You can achieve a gossamer effect for transparent insect wings by using a very delicate touch on the veins and slightly emphasizing these at the joins. Use only a very diluted off-white wash for the wings, just enough so that when the picture is washed, the wing will be very delicately differentiated from the background color. If you can find Chinese gold paint, use it to enhance butterfly wings.

Freestyle method
While outline insects are relatively simple to paint, freestyle insects can cause problems because they must be done with the minimum of strokes and the maximum of panache. For the bees shown at right, put in

the head, eyes, and stripes first. Fill your brush with yellow and tip it in a mixture of burnt sienna and vermilion. Lay the brush over the back stripe with the tip toward the head. Press down lightly and immediately lift the brush cleanly off the paper. Then add the legs and antennae. Feather your brush and put in the wing veins, remembering that the front pair of wings is larger than the rear pair. To paint the wings, fill your brush with very diluted white and

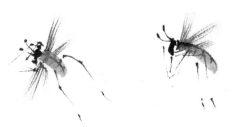

Freestyle bees.

73

press down once for each wing with the tip toward the body.

For the dragonfly pictured below, begin by putting in the head with a firm "bone" stroke. It is best to use a horsehair brush, although a plum blossom brush will do. Next, do the neck and thorax without taking the brush off the paper. Continue straight on to the body, which is done with a stop/start stroke similar to that for a small freestyle bamboo stem. Taper the last segment. Add the legs with light but very firm strokes, going back slightly on yourself at the joints. Remember that most insects have six legs and that one pair is often more prominent than the others. Add the antennae. Paint the wings with a dry brush and very light ink, starting at the body and

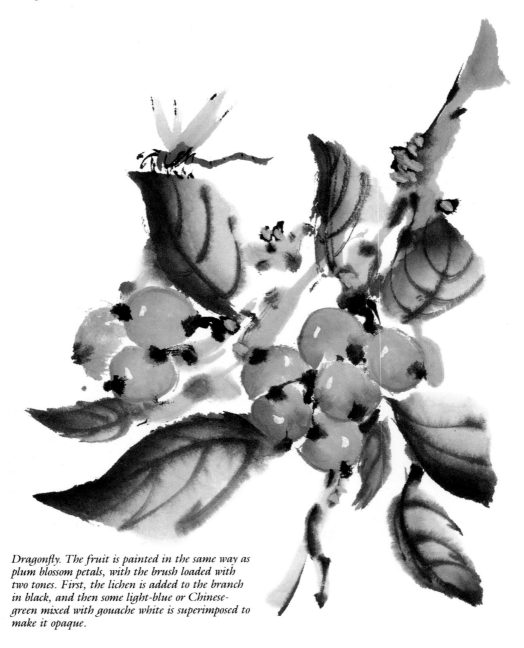

Dragonfly. The fruit is painted in the same way as plum blossom petals, with the brush loaded with two tones. First, the lichen is added to the branch in black, and then some light-blue or Chinese-green mixed with gouache white is superimposed to make it opaque.

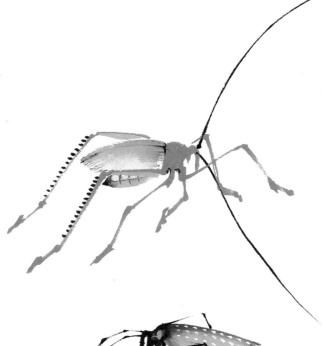

beetle are done with a stroke similar to that for the dragonfly's body.

The principles of painting the praying mantis below are essentially the same, but change the shape of the thorax and angle the wing more sharply than for the beetles. Make the antennae especially long and try to make them look as if they are waving about. Notice the shapes of the legs: the front ones should be prominent since they give the creature its name.

The butterflies on page 76, top are slightly different because you do not start with the head but with the wings. Fill a

Praying Mantis. *Space is again used here as a compositional element.*

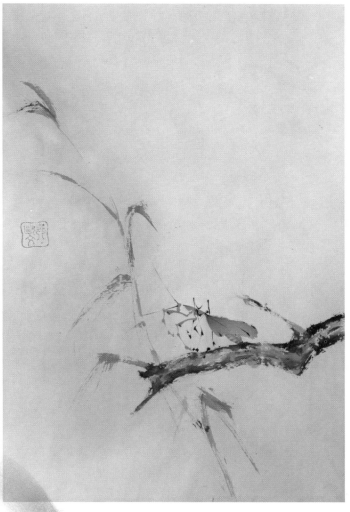

Beetles.

pulling the brush upward and sideways to achieve the ragged edge. Then add the small black marks at the tips of the wings.

The head and thorax of the beetles shown above are done like the dragonfly's. For the wing section, fill your brush with the required color, dipping half the length of the bristles in a slightly darker tone. Position your brush on the paper with the tip against the top of the thorax and the heel at a slight angle to the right. Press down lightly while simultaneously pulling the brush sideways, then lift it as you make the stroke until the brush has left the paper. Next, fill your brush with the two tones you are using for the body and lay it on the paper with the tip toward the tail. Press down the heel and immediately lift the brush cleanly off the paper. Add the legs, making sure they all come from the thorax and adding black hairs or thickening them as called for by the species of beetle. The antennae on the top

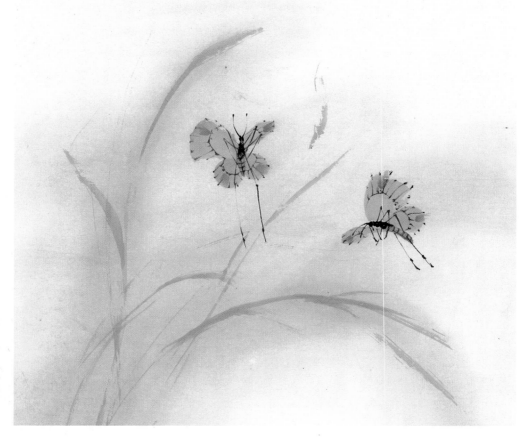

Butterflies. *All the wings are completed without taking the brush off the paper.*

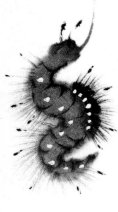

*Caterpillar
spinning
a cocoon.*

plum blossom brush with a light color and tip it with a darker tone. Place the full length of the brush at the outside edge of the largest wing, then, keeping the whole of the brush in contact with the paper, pull the brush toward where the body will be. Without taking the brush off the paper, draw it backward along the bristles and make a circle for the second wing, using a stroke similar to that you would use for a plum blossom petal. Still without taking the brush off the paper, pull the tip across and make another smaller circular wing, then draw the brush up and out to make the fourth wing. At the last moment, press down lightly with the heel of your brush and then lift it off cleanly. While the wings are still wet, add the two-tone splotches. The head and

thorax are painted in black and the body in an appropriate color. Paint in the legs and antennae and put veins on the wings, remembering to emphasize lightly the points where the veins meet.

At left is a caterpillar or silkworm spinning a cocoon. The basic shape of the body is painted in a light tone with a single, twisting motion of the brush. While this is still wet, pull the feathered strokes out with a split brush, then add the darker area and feather it. Indicate the head with a slightly darker tone and, using black, put in the feelers and the striped markings. Touch the ends of a few of the spines with dark color as you did for the joins on the butterfly's wing markings. Then add the white spots.

Although they are not strictly insects, it

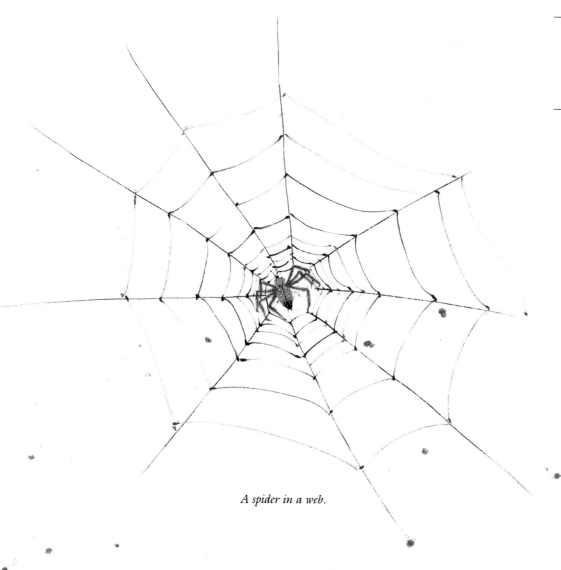

A spider in a web.

seems appropriate to include spiders in this section. Do the head first, followed by the thorax and the body. The legs are painted with firm strokes that are then feathered. Add the feelers last. If you put your spider on a web, you must make the web look as if it could support the spider's weight, so keep the strands straight. Emphasize the joints in the same way as you do when putting veins on an insect's wing.

Common mistakes
By far the most common difficulties in painting insects result from a lack of under-

standing of their shapes and proportions. Students often elongate the bodies, make the heads too small, or put them too near the thorax. They also have a tendency to make wings too small and legs insubstantial and hesitant, so be careful when painting these. Make sure, too, that you join the legs and wings in the right places. Another common mistake is to make the color too thin. It's important to use fairly thick paint and a dryish brush; otherwise your insect will look insubstantial rather than delicate. Study insects closely; you may be surprised to discover that even spiders are fascinating.

PAINTING FISH AND OTHER AQUATIC CREATURES

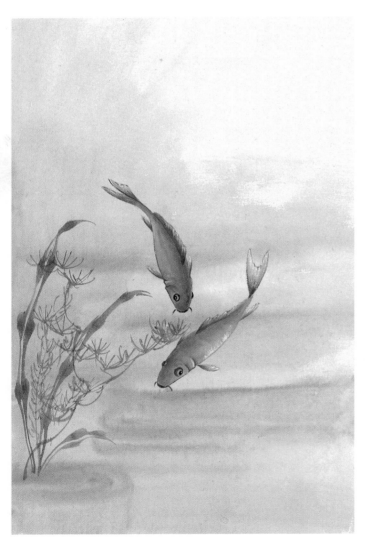

Although they are less common in Chinese painting than birds, fish have been a constant theme. They are often thought to represent abundance and the regeneration of life, and a pair of fish can symbolize sexual union.

Gongbi-style fish

For the fish shown here, outline the shapes lightly in gray ink, starting at the head and putting in only the main line for each of the fins. Then clean your brush and put a stripe of water down the length of the body, taking care to cover only about the center third. Fill your brush with light gray ink, remembering to wipe off any excess on the side of the palette, and tip it with black ink. Placing the brush so that the darkest ink comes along the spine of your fish and the lighter tone in the heel of the brush runs into the damp area, run the color into the outline, beginning at the head but avoiding the eyes. Wash your brush thoroughly and then fill it with diluted gouache white, tipping the end in concentrated white. This time, position the brush so that the tip runs along the belly of your fish and the diluted white on the heel runs into the damp area. Rinse your brush and blend the two colors together.

You will have to do the gills separately, although the method is the same. The fins and the tail are also done in a similar way but without any preliminary wetting of the

Fish. *For these* gongbi *fish, color is blended from dark to light—the only time this is done.*

paper. For the fins, put the darkest color along your guide lines; for the tail, put it at the base where the tail joins the body. Finally, paint in the eyes and the eye areas and add a few white and black markings to the fins and tail.

You will notice that the normal rules about blending from light to dark are reversed for fish—the only occasion this happens. This is because the diluted white over the gray gives a silvery effect that is highly desirable when trying to suggest fish scales under water. The chapter on washes (see page 115) explains how to achieve the water effect. For the frondy weeds, use a stroke similar to that used for pine needles. Of course, you can substitute a color for gray when doing this kind of fish.

The fish shown below are done by the same method, but before you add the shading or color you draw more detail and put in the scales. In **a**, you do this with just a fine line, but in **b** you also add some gray shading and black spots for the breathing line down the side of the fish. Obviously, fish vary widely in color and shape, but the same basic method applies in most cases.

Xieyi-style fish
Two styles of freestyle fish are illustrated on page 80. The figure on the left shows Lingnam-style fish, which are begun by drawing the front of the mouth and the eye bulges in black. Add the gills in gray and then, using very light ink, mark in the backbone. Still using light ink, put in the line of the belly by positioning the tip of your brush at the point where the gill turns upward and pulling it back along the line of the belly. Keeping the angle of the bristles the same, make the upward stroke at the back of the belly with the side of the brush. Still without

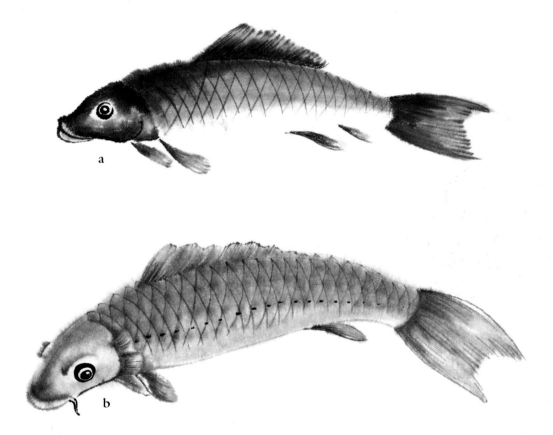

Detailed fish with their scales drawn in lightly before the shading or color is added.

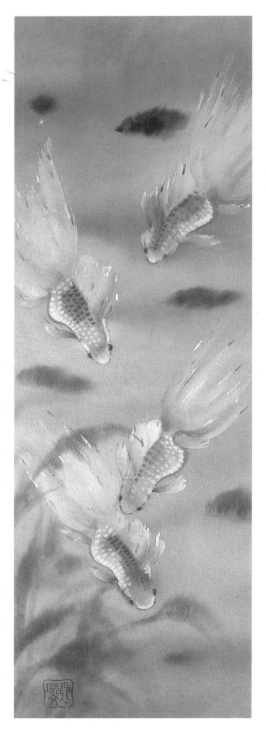

Goldfish. *Lingnam-style goldfish, with reeds
added while the wash is still wet (private
collection).*

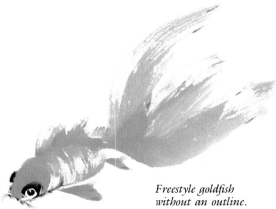

*Freestyle goldfish
without an outline.*

taking the brush off the paper or altering its
angle, follow the line around to make the
lower edge of the tail, tapering the stroke.
Then add the other side of the tail. Mark the
fins as you did on page 78.

Next, wet the center of the body area.
Paint in the dark colors on the body using
rich, bright color on the tip of your brush
and pressing down with more diluted color
in the heel so that the colors blend with
each other and run slightly into the dampened central area. The colors are usually
variegated: orange, yellow, and red or
brown, red, and black. The lighter portions
of the head and body are done with white,
thicker on the belly as for the fish on page
78. Highlight the gills with white and the
eye bulges with sky blue.

The side fins are done by loading the
brush with varying tones and stroking on
each fin in one motion, starting with the
brush tip against the body and pulling outward. The dorsal (back) fin is done by
loading the brush with the same tones and
positioning it sideways along the backbone
with the tip toward the head. Pull the brush
upward with a sideways stroke, at first keeping the whole brush in contact with the
paper but then, as you move upward, gradually lifting it off, starting with the heel.
For the tail, once again load your brush
with the same tones and use a side stroke,
but in reverse: begin with only the tip of the
brush in contact with the paper at the point
where the tail joins the body and gradually
press down the heel as you move the brush
outward, keeping the bristles at right angles
to the direction of your movement. Once
you are using the full length of the bristles,

start to lift the brush off the paper, continuing the stroke into the air. Two strokes like this should be enough to complete the tail. Then, add the splotches of color on the fins and tail and some light veining in color and white, together with the scale dots.

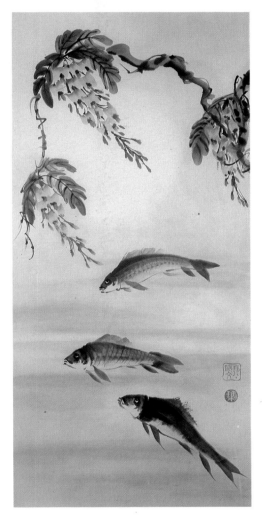

Fish with Wisteria. *The scale markings are added to the fish while the paper is still wet by putting in fine criss-cross lines and dabbing a hint of shading into the scales. The flowers of the wisteria are done first, using a loaded brush and painting the main petals with an inward, sideways stroke. Then, the darker, smaller petals and the stalks are added. The central veins for the leaves are put in next, using the shape of the brush pressed onto the paper to form the leaf sections. The other veins are added last, and then the branch and tendrils are put in.*

In contrast, the freestyle goldfish on page 80 is done without an outline, using a method that can be adapted effectively to different shapes (see figure at left). Begin by putting in the eye and its surrounding area, then add the mouth and the gills. Load your brush with light ink and half fill it with dark ink. To fill in the body, place the brush so that the tip is pointing toward the top of the head and the bristles are lying along the backbone, and start to pull it back to the tail, almost immediately stroking it downward in a rounded movement to shape the flank. Add a light dry line to suggest the

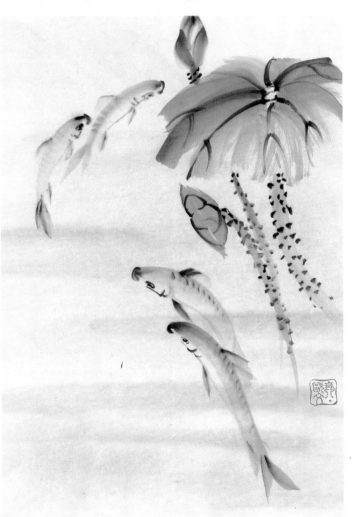

Fish and Lotus. *This is painted on wet paper. The illusion of water is created by the use of space.*

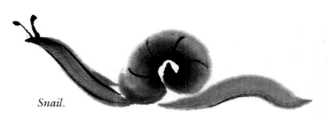

Snail.

belly. Paint the tail and fins as you did for the Lingnam-style goldfish, but without first putting in a guide line.

In the illustration on page 81, right, wet paper was used so that the bodies of the fish would blend into the background. In this case, you should paint the head first, followed by the body, fins, and tail. Add the eyes and gills last. Remember to load the brush from light to dark as before, but this time create the body of the fish by pulling your brush along its bristles rather than across them.

Other aquatic creatures

While we are on the subject of fish, it seems logical to deal with other aquatic creatures that have become increasingly popular among contemporary Chinese painters.

To paint the crabs shown below, fill your brush with light gray and tip it in dark ink. Paint the central section of the shell with a downward stroke using the side of the brush; the side segments are added in the

same way. Then put in the pincers and the eyes. Then, add the legs, using a bamboo stem stroke but tapering the feet sections.

For the shrimp illustrated on page 134, begin with the head by doing two strokes with the brush tip toward the head and the heel pressed down. Next, put in the body segments and the tail, then add the eyes, mouth, tentacles, legs, and pincers.

For the turtle illustrated on page 10, put in the light shading for the shell first and then the shading for the head. (Remember your technique for branches and rocks.) While the gray ink is still wet, add the shell markings and the legs in a darker tone, then pick out the face in black.

Although the snail, shown above, is not normally regarded as an aquatic animal, it seems to fit most readily into this section. Do the shell first, in a light tone, beginning in the middle and gradually increasing brush contact as you progress. Add the head and body and then put in the markings and the eye stalks. If you want, you can also include a trail mark by wetting the paper and putting in a faint line where the snail has been.

The frog right will probably cause you more trouble than the crab and the shrimp. Put in the eye first. Then load your brush with a base of dirty green and a tip of dark red. Place the tip of the brush to make the mouth and press down for the head, moving the heel slightly to make the eye bulge. Without taking the brush off the paper, lift the heel as you pull the brush backward to make the neck. Still with the brush on the paper, press down firmly again with the heel and move it gently to either side to make the back. Add the legs by using only one stroke for each, but vary the pressure in order to achieve the thickening for the thighs and calves, and splay the ends to create the webbed effect by pressing the brush down quickly, then lifting it cleanly off the paper.

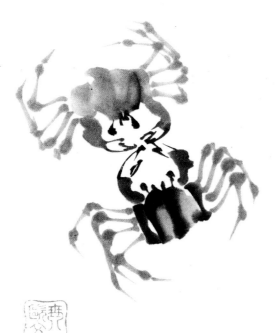

Crabs. This picture is done in the style of Qi Baishi, perhaps the best-known twentieth-century Chinese painter. Once again a simple subject painted with the minimum of brush strokes makes a satisfyingly complete composition.

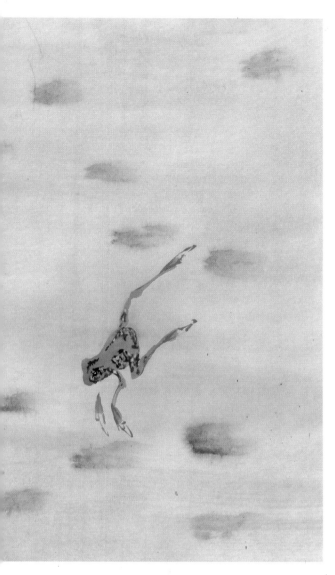

For the belly, load your brush with light color and tip it in darker. Position the brush so that the tip forms the chin and pull backward, pressing down with the heel to form a rounded shape. Use dark red to add the toes and black for the markings, which must be put in while the painting is wet. Add gouache yellow or light green to some of the black spots. Surround the bottom of the eye with orange and put a gouache yellow stripe above it.

When putting a wash on a painting of aquatic creatures (see page 117), it is helpful to apply it to the front of the picture to add to the illusion that the animals are beneath the water. Adding reeds and lily pads before the wash has dried (see page 71) also enhances the watery effect.

Common mistakes
A common mistake beginners make when painting outlined fishes is using white too thickly, with the result that their fish look heavy, lifeless, and not at all watery. Head shape sometimes causes trouble, too; beware of making your fish look like dolphins! Shape causes problems in freestyle paintings as well, especially in Lingnam-style fish; heads tend to become very narrow and bodies elongate alarmingly. You may also have difficulty with color running when doing fish, but do not worry about this too much unless you find you are losing the shapes. A little blurring round the edges of your fish adds to the watery effect.

Painting crabs and shrimp presents few difficulties, although crab legs sometimes wander rather indecisively. Try not to use too many strokes when doing frogs.

Frog. *The lily pads are added before the wash is completely dry.*

PAINTING BIRDS

It is perhaps in *gongbi* paintings of birds that the drawbacks of the Chinese habit of copying show up most clearly. Although they are often decorative, birds in Chinese paintings are frequently static and occasionally anatomically inaccurate. In paintings of birds, artists have shown a tendency to concentrate on using the correct brush stroke at the expense of conveying the nature of the subject. There are, of course, many very beautiful *gongbi* bird paintings, some of which would grace any bird watcher's manual for accuracy. However, they sometimes lack that essential element of movement that is so extraordinarily well captured by successful *xieyi* bird painting. You can avoid some of the pitfalls of overstylization by remembering the moral of the story about the painters of the ducks (see page 19). Look at birds; see how they fly, land, perch, and eat.

Small birds: *gongbi* style

As you will see from the illustration below, *gongbi*-method birds should first be drawn with a fine-pointed brush. Start by drawing the eye and the beak in black ink. With gray ink and a feathered brush, lightly outline the head. Next, put in the black wing feathers with a bamboo leaf stroke. Again with gray and a feathered brush, add the back and the breast. Then put in the tail and the legs. Obviously the shape of the bird should be varied according to the species, as should

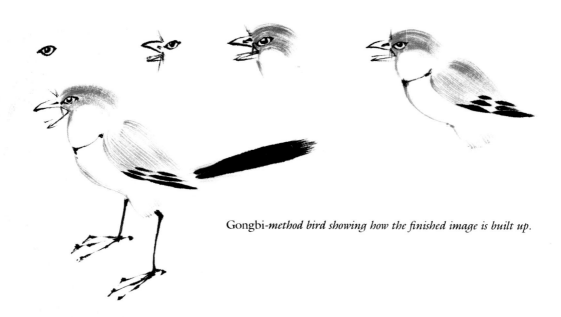

Gongbi-method bird showing how the finished image is built up.

84

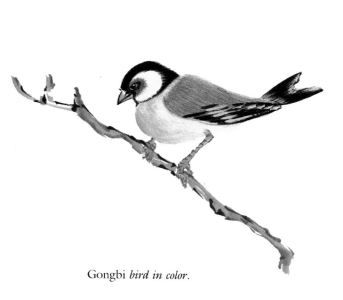

Gongbi *bird in color*.

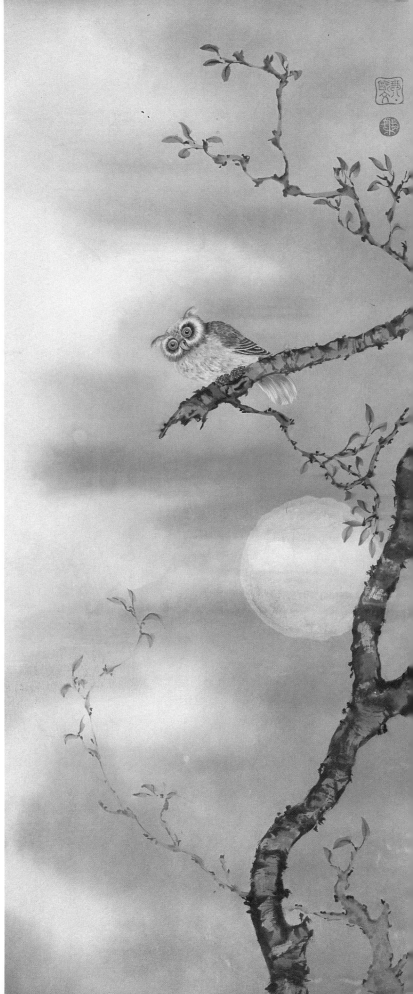

the coloring, which, as you will by now expect in a *gongbi* painting, is done by blending. Remember to blend from light to dark. After you have filled in the basic colors, put in markings such as the little crossbars on the wings. Add a touch of white to the eye to bring it alive. If you want to give your bird a speckled breast, fill a small brush with the predominant light color you want and tip it in a darker tone, then use it with a dabbing motion, overlapping your strokes. The painting above shows a *gongbi* small bird in color.

Large birds: *gongbi* style
In the illustrations at right and on page 86, left, large birds are treated in a detailed manner—the method is essentially the same as for small birds. You should always begin by outlining the eye and the beak and then draw in the head, wings, back, breast, tail, legs, and feet. The peacock on page 16 was also painted in this way.

Some large birds are painted in meticulous detail, with many of their feathers put in individually. A selection of different feathers is illustrated on page 86. In each case, start by marking in the spine in light ink. Using a small split brush, work outward from the spine with a feather stroke.

Owl. *This is painted in the* gongbi-*method and shows the use of the speckled technique. The moon is painted in white gouache on the reverse side of the painting so that when the wash is added to the front, the illusion of clouds floating in front of the moon is achieved. The sky effect is created by applying a graduated wash.*

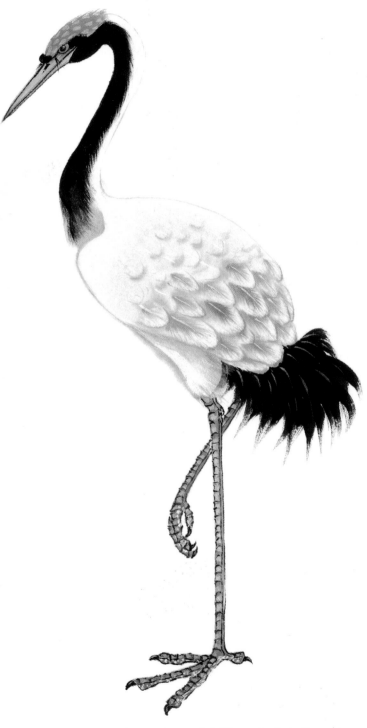

Then reverse the stroke and feather inward from the outer edge. Next, add a wash of the predominant color of the bird. Emphasize the spine with black and highlight it with white if this is appropriate to the coloring of your bird. You may also need to highlight the edge of the feather. This basic method for painting feathers can be adapted for most shapes, color schemes, and sizes.

Normally the breasts of birds are painted with blended colors and do not have the feathers marked individually, although ducks are sometimes an exception to this rule. The crane's tail (left) is done with sweeping bamboo leaf strokes. When painting a peacock, as illustrated on page 16, it is advisable to establish the overall shape of the tail by marking the tail feathers lightly in gray. If you cannot obtain any Chinese or Japanese gold paint for these feathers, you can use gold plaka. However, you will have to add this after the picture has been

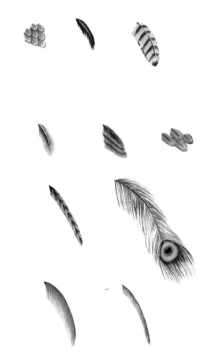

A selection of feathers. A small, split-brush should be used for the smaller feathers; for the larger ones, it is more effective to apply very fine, tapered, individual strokes with the tip of a small brush.

A crane is a symbol of longevity that often occurs in paintings, alongside pine trees.

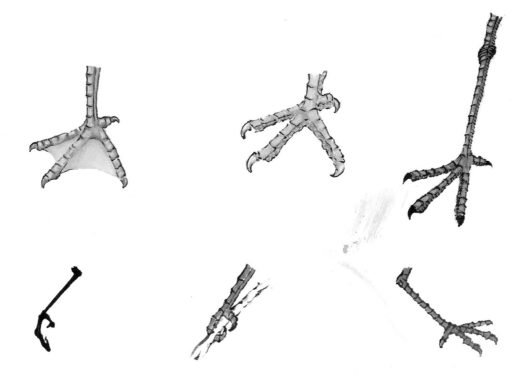

mounted because it tends to wash off otherwise. Above are some examples of the legs and feet of birds also done by this detailed method.

Small birds: *xieyi* style
Watching birds is essential if you are going to paint freestyle ones that successfully convey movement and life. Small freestyle birds are begun by painting either the belly or the back, depending on the angle of the bird. For the bird below, take a soft sheep-, goat-, or rabbit-hair brush and saturate it in the light breast color. Tip the brush with darker

Birds' legs and feet. These would usually be painted in color. Spots of gouache white or gouache white mixed with yellow are applied before the overall color of the leg or foot is added, creating a spotted effect. Highlighting on the front sections of the legs and on the tops of the feet should be blended in on top of the color.

Small xieyi *bird showing how the creature is built up beginning with the breast. It is vital to do a* xieyi *bird in one breath so that the colors blend. It is equally important to have strong black ink and good color tones if you want your bird to look lively.*

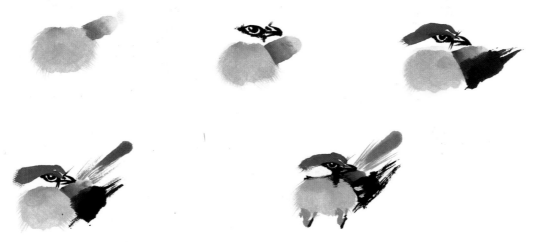

color, then place it so that the darker tone will come at the chin and press down firmly on the paper, moving the brush to make the shape of the bird's chest. Try to do this in one movement. Lift the brush and split it, then feather the edges of the breast. Fill your brush with a darker color and paint the shoulder area of the back with a sideways stroke. When you have done this, change to a firmer brush, preferably a horsehair one, and put in the eye and the beak with bold strokes. For the top of the head, fill your brush with ink or color and place it so that the tip forms the front of the face above the beak. Lay the brush down firmly, turning it

slightly so that the heel meets the shoulder. Make a second stroke for the top of the head in the same manner, but this time include a small bump above the eye by moving the brush sideways slightly while you are laying it down. You should never use more than two strokes for the top of the head. Do the wing next with a bold side stroke, augmented by one or two pushed vertical strokes, then add the tail. Paint the markings around the eye and those on the cheek, chest, head, and wings. Color the beak and put in the tongue if the mouth is open. Highlight the eye with a dab of white, and also fill in the cheek with white if appropriate. Then add the feet.

The bird at left is done by exactly the same method except the back is painted first with the soft brush. The feathering technique should be used not to puff up the chest but to pull the stroke backward, providing the base of the tail. The black tail feather is done with a stroke pushed outward from the body. Do the head as before. Leave the chest until after you have put in the chin area and the wings. Note that birds seen from this angle show more leg than those seen face on. Some examples of legs and feet suitable for small birds are shown on page 89.

As with *gongbi* birds, you can vary the shape, size, and coloring according to the species. It is important to pay particular

Small xieyi *bird painted by completing the back first.*

88

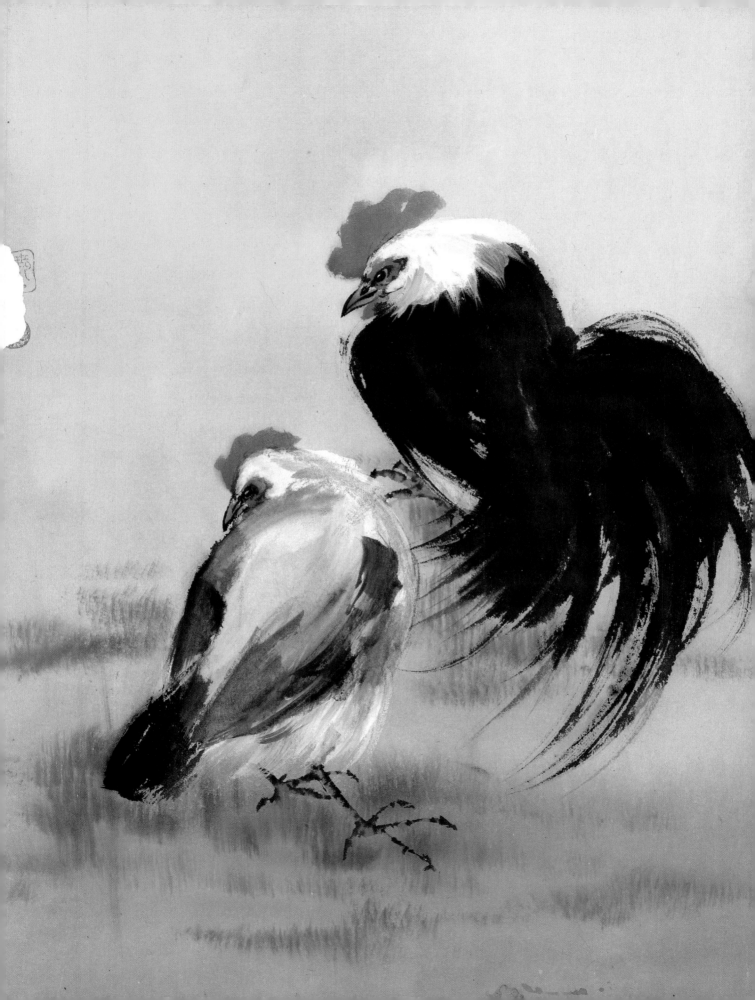

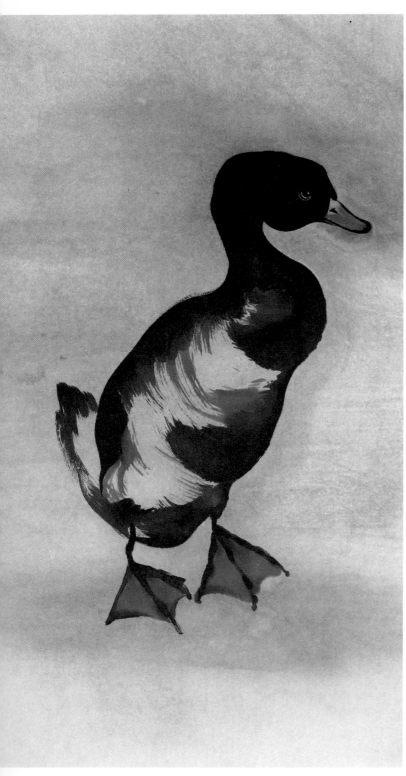

The duck at left is entirely done with a large wolf-hair brush. Begin with the eye and the beak and then paint the head, using a fluid movement of the brush, which must stay in contact with the paper. Do the body in the same way. Add the wing and tail markings with darker ink, and put in the feet last.

The bird of prey (opposite) combines the techniques of the outline method used for the egret and the totally freestyle method used for the cock and ducks. For instance, the head is done by the egret method, whereas the feet are done like the cock's feet. The wings, back, and tail are painted with sweeping side strokes of your largest brush, preferably a horsehair one. The leg is done with free feathered strokes.

Common mistakes

By far the most common problem people have with outline-method birds is with the legs and feet. Remember to make the feet large enough to support the bird—birds have surprisingly large feet—and make sure the legs look firm and strong. Remember, too, that birds have chests, not stomachs; beginners often make them look eggbound! Pay attention to the positioning of eyes and beaks, and keep the tops of the heads fairly flat. Above all, do not be in too much of a hurry, especially if you are painting a large bird; haste results in messy-looking feathers. Treat the portrayal of a detailed bird as a labor of love and be meticulous about each feather.

With small *xieyi* birds the problems are more varied, but shape, legs, and feet again cause a large proportion of them. Make sure you keep the weight distribution up in the chest area and not in the belly, and use firm, bold strokes for the legs and feet. Another very common mistake with freestyle birds is using too many strokes. Remember, use only one stroke for the back and one for the breast, two strokes at most for the top of the head, and a maximum of three for the wing. Overworking a freestyle bird destroys its spontaneity and robs it of its main attraction, which is movement. You must also make sure that your ink is

This duck is painted with the fewest possible number of strokes.

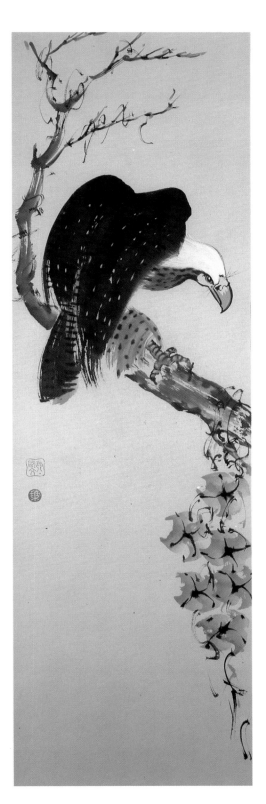

thick and black and that your colors are bright and bold; beginners often use rather watery tones.

Large freestyle birds do not seem to cause as many problems as small ones, although there is often a tendency to make them too neat and tidy. You must always use bold strokes and, as with the small birds, rich black ink and strong colors.

Bird of Prey after Hau Chiok. *This shows how different techniques can be successfully combined in one painting.*

PAINTING MAMMALS

The approximate association of *gongbi* with the outline method breaks down completely when it comes to mammals. Although you can naturally portray any animal you want by drawing it in outline with a fine-pointed brush, traditionally Chinese painters have hardly ever depicted animals in outline. It is the meticulous detailing of fur and other markings that usually distinguishes a *gongbi* animal painting from a *xieyi* one. The exceptions to this rule are the famous *gongbi* paintings of horses done by Giuseppe Castiglione, which were done in outline first. Generally with animals, however, the line between *gongbi* and *xieyi* is hard to determine.

Remember to watch animals as you do birds. Observation is by far the most useful technique you have. You should by now be able to work out for yourself how to tackle an animal by outlining it, so we will not go into detail again here. Concentrate on making the shape of the beast natural and strive for a feeling of movement. Remember that a feathered stroke can suggest fur as easily as it can feathers or grass. For outlined animals, use the lessons in coloring that you learned for fish and birds.

Horses

Horses have always been an important theme in Chinese painting. Even the Yuan dynasty (*c.* 1279–1368), which was not remarkable for its painting, produced a very fine calligrapher, Zhao Mengfu, who is equally remembered for his pictures of horses. To the Chinese, the horse stands for perseverance and speed. The method of painting them is reminiscent of that used for depicting rocks and branches in that the shading is put in first to create form and the outline is added afterward.

For the horse shown opposite, begin with the shading of the head and neck. Add the belly with an upward movement of the side of the brush. Shade the rump and the tops of the legs where appropriate. Then reload your brush with black ink and outline the horse with free-flowing strokes. The lower part of each leg should be done with a single stroke in the "bone" manner. Next, add the hooves and ears, and last, put in the mane and tail, using the minimum of strokes and the maximum of dash.

Other mammals

Furrier animals, such as those shown on pages 96–101, should also have the shading done first, but no outline is added. Instead, the rest of the body is completed with a light wash. The detail is picked out in black, and the furry texture added with a feathered brush. You may find it easier to sketch your animal lightly in charcoal as you did with the large freestyle birds until you become practiced at knowing where to put your wash. You can also achieve a very furry effect, should you so desire, by wetting the paper before you begin. If you do this, however, you would be well advised to leave details like the eye and the mouth until after you have applied the wash because it will then be easier to position them properly.

When you are painting furry animals, you may like to reflect that several of them have symbolic meanings and beliefs attached to them. The rat, for example, can be an emblem of timidity and meanness, but on the other hand it is also seen as representing industry and prosperity. The tiger is

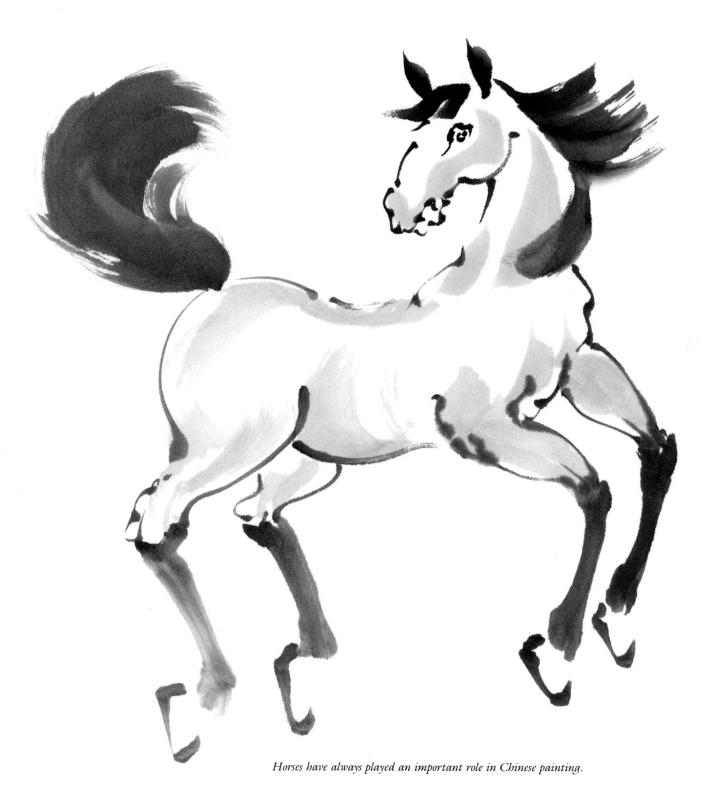

Horses have always played an important role in Chinese painting.

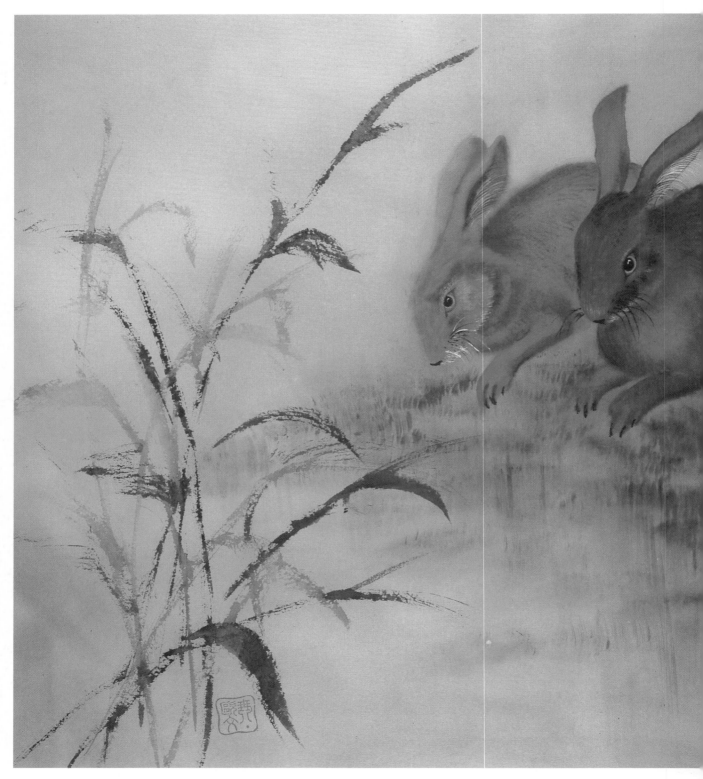

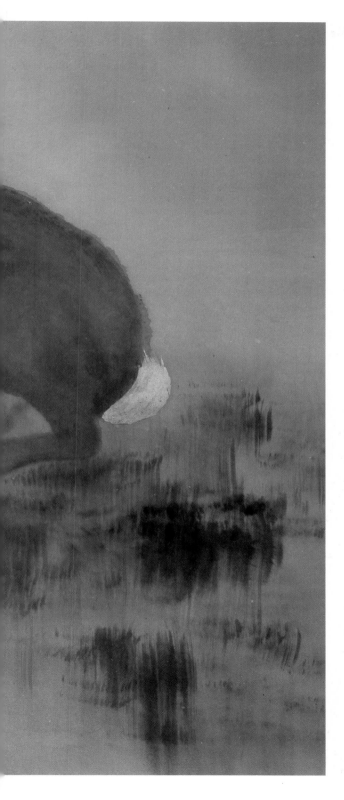

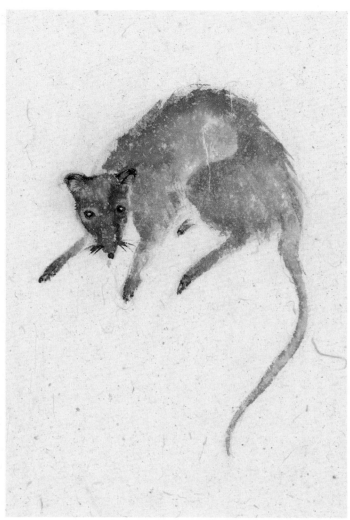

Rat. *The basic shape is worked wet and then drier texture is added to the fur with a rough brush or a twisted wolf-hair one.*

Baby Rabbits. *These are worked on wet paper to create the soft, furry effect (private collection).*

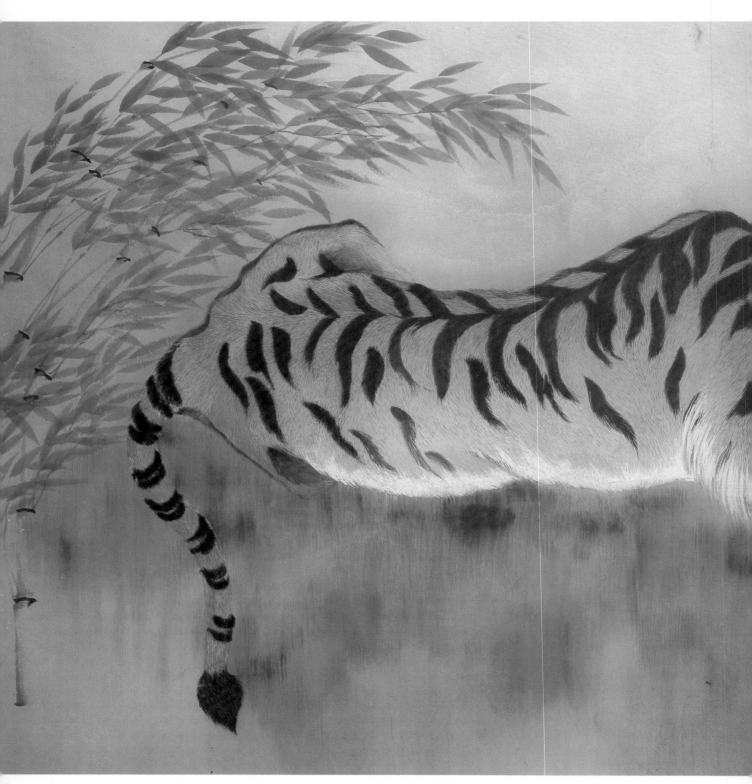

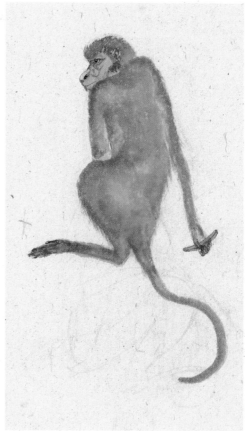

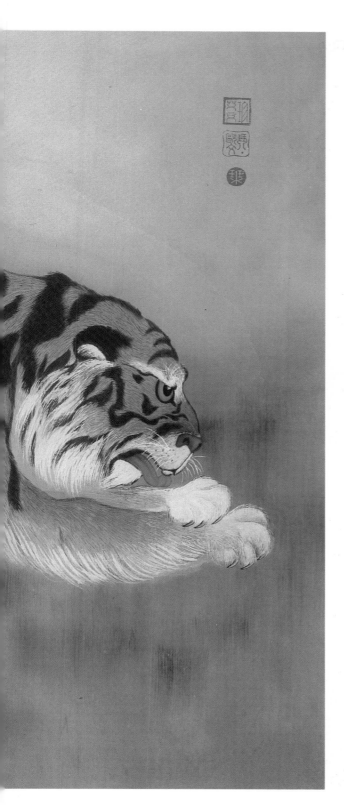

Monkey. *The texture of fur is created by applying gray and black shading on damp paper, slowly, so that it spreads and blurs.*

Tiger. *Again the basic shape is worked on damp paper, but this time the fur is added much more painstakingly with feathered strokes of a good wolf-hair brush and different colors. The texture of the wash is achieved by applying dry color with a wash brush before the overall wash has completely dried.*

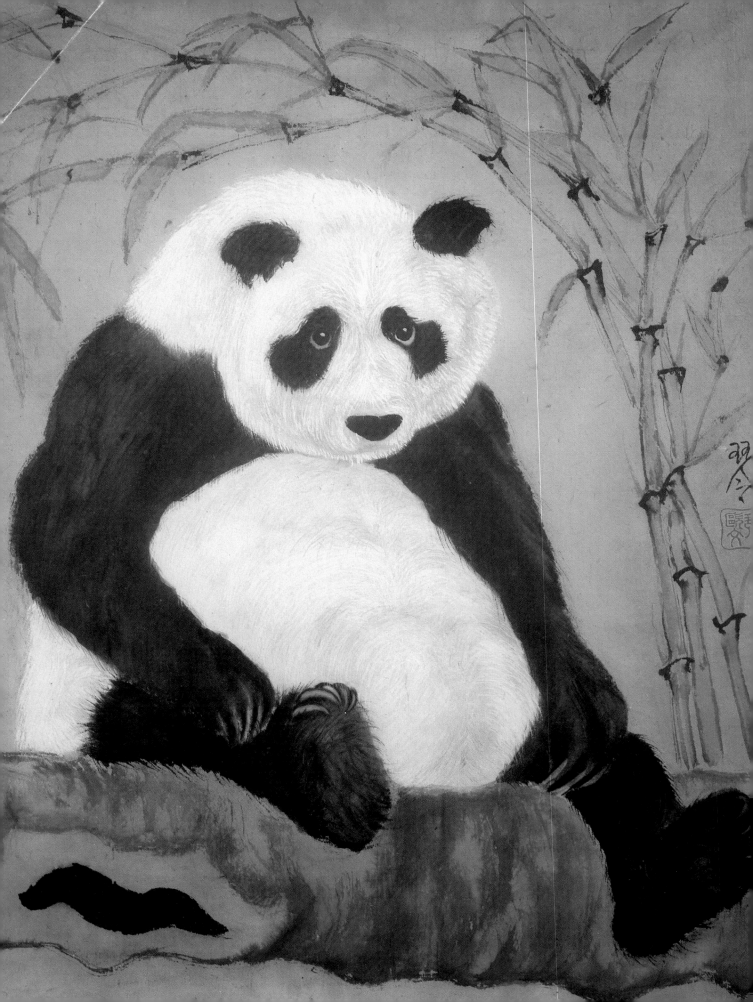

Panda. *The shading in the white sections is applied first. Then, a white wash is slowly applied so that it "furs." White highlights are added by blending in denser white, and some feathered strokes are superimposed for additional furry texture. The black sections are worked wet and then drier texture is added to the fur with a rough brush (private collection).*

This panda is more typical than the one shown at left. It is worked on dry paper by applying the ink with slow, steady pressure to create a furry effect.

regarded as the king of beasts; it is dignified and stern as well as ferocious and daring. The monkey represents ugliness and trickery and is believed to control witches and hobgoblins; it is also, however, an object of worship, particularly for the sick or the unsuccessful. The cat is seen as rather an unlucky emblem. The coming of a cat to a house is thought to signal the coming of poverty, so it is perhaps not surprising that the cat does not feature very largely in Chinese painting, although it occurs from time to time.

For some animals brush strokes are used to provide outline and body simultaneously. Each stroke has to be carefully placed in such a way as to give form to the

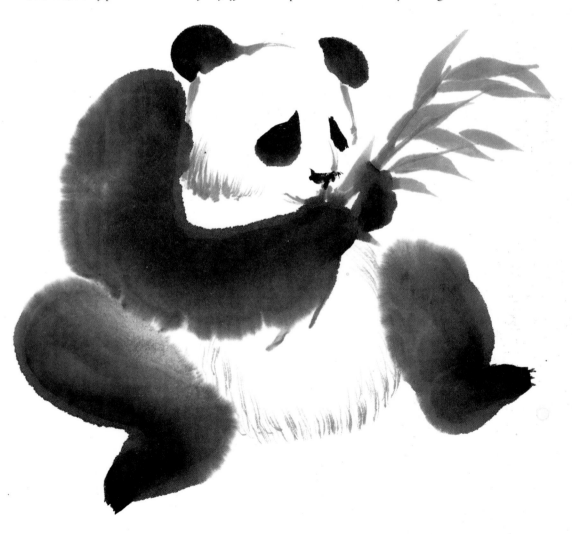

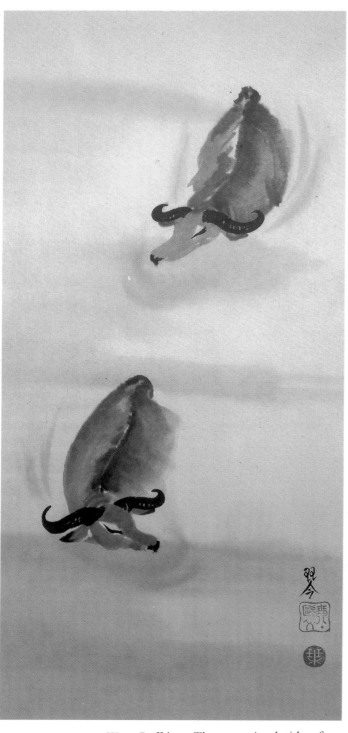

animal. The cat and mouse illustrated on page 14 and the panda on page 101 are done on dry paper. They are made to look furry by using a wet brush and by working the body shapes slowly so that the ink spreads. For the cat, put in the shapes of the head, ears, body, legs, and tail, leaving spaces for the eyes. Add the dark markings while the gray is still wet. Finally, put in the details of the eyes, whiskers, nose, and mouth. For the mouse, do the head, body, tail, and ears in gray, using one stroke for each. Add the black details. For the panda, first place the eye patches with single strokes. Then, add the ears and the black areas and with a split brush outline the white parts with gray ink.

The water buffaloes are done by the same method but with a slightly drier brush and working faster to avoid too much furring. Start with the head and, leaving spaces for the eyes and horns, lay down each stroke carefully, keeping the animal's shape clear. Add the eyes, horns, nose, and other details in black. Use as few strokes as possible, preferably only one for each section of the animals. Have enough ink on your brush to complete the stroke. The chapter on washes explains how to represent water and its movement.

Common mistakes
Most of the mistakes beginners make when painting mammals are caused by our old favorites: overworking—too many strokes will destroy animation; and lack of observation—this will result in unlikely shapes.

Water Buffaloes. *These are painted with as few strokes as possible on dry paper.*

PAINTING PEOPLE

Unlike other mammals, people are almost always depicted in outline. This is true of both *gongbi* and *xieyi* paintings. For *gongbi*-style figures, follow the instructions for flower painting, remembering to use a clean, fine line for the outline and to blend the color carefully. Traditional paintings of people seldom show any shading on the face and usually none on the clothing, but if you wish you can blend shadows into robes and even on faces, as illustrated below.

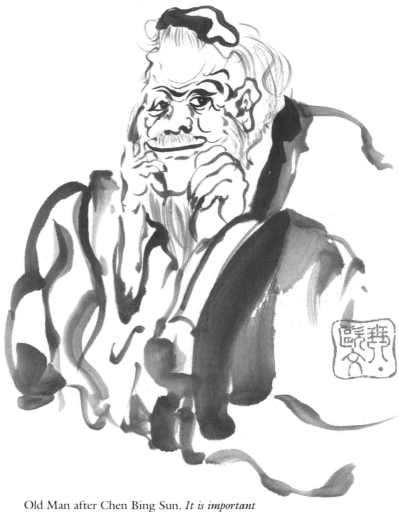

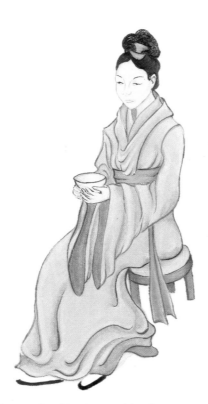

Figure painted in the gongbi *style.*

Old Man after Chen Bing Sun. *It is important when "drawing" with the brush, as for the face, to vary the pressure if you want to achieve texture and liveliness.*

103

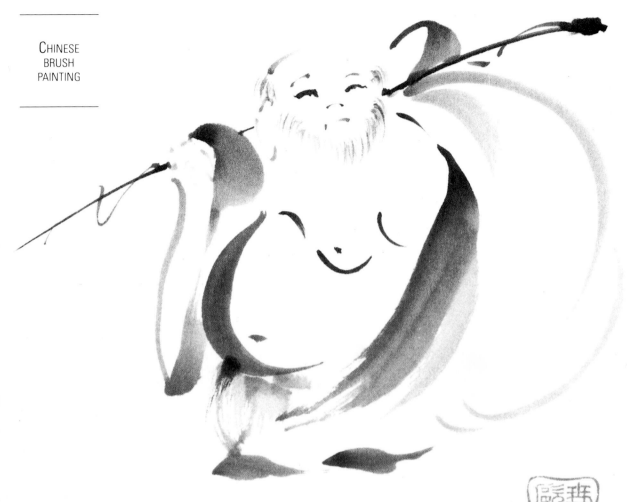

Xieyi figures do not have shadows, however. They are done with expressive brush strokes and any color is added as a very light wash. The paintings reproduced here and on page 103, right, are examples of this technique. The one shown above is a copy of the Hotei, or god of fortune, a figure more commonly encountered in Japanese painting. However, the strokes used for this Sumi rendition are the same as for Chinese black and white *xieyi* painting.

Hotei after Hakuho Hirayama. *The Hotei, or god of fortune, is a Japanese figure, but this example shows the clear relationship between Japanese Sumi painting and Chinese ink painting.*

PAINTING LANDSCAPES

There are probably more conventions governing the painting of landscapes in the Chinese tradition than for any other subject. Indeed, in the past painters have occasionally become bogged down by these conventions and have looked to earlier eras of painting in the hope of returning to a style relatively untrammeled by rules and prohibitions.

Apart from the monk artists of the Song dynasty (*c.* 960–1279), landscape painters have usually enjoyed the highest status among artists. In the past, scholar painters were the only ones who thought it was worthwhile to travel to look at actual scenery, and even they gave a fairly low priority to accuracy in their paintings of landscapes. Until comparatively recently, Chinese painters have not seen it as their role to provide a representational image. As with other subjects, they seek to convey the spirit of their subject. They have in fact sought to remain detached from painting specific localities, feeling that this might interfere with their efforts to convey spirituality. In Chinese philosophy great emphasis is laid on meditation and retreat. Quite obviously society could not function if all its officials and rulers pursued this ideal to its logical conclusion and retired from life to indulge in solitary meditation somewhere in the wilderness, so painters in dynastic China provided imaginary scenes for people to retreat into by contemplation. Traditionally, therefore, subjects in Academic pictures were edifying, and landscape painting became the most prestigious art form.

Landscape painting perhaps shows the most obvious changes in recent years. Many modern Chinese painters use Western perspective and have abandoned many of the conventions. Nevertheless, the landscape painting that is being done in China today and by Chinese painters in the West represents very much a development of the traditions and not their abrogation. An understanding of these traditions is therefore necessary for the learner.

Traditions in landscape painting

Traditionally, Chinese artists have treated perspective quite differently from Western artists. Their paintings have no vanishing point. The overall scene is viewed as if from above, while the elements in it are viewed from the side. You may, for example, have a tree in the foreground growing as if you were standing on the same level as it is. Above it you may have a mountain that is obviously behind the tree from your viewpoint but which is placed on top of it in the painting. Curiously, the only individual element of a picture that is usually depicted as if from above is a building. Trees and figures beside the building, however, are seen face or side on.

Similarly—and this holds for all Chinese painting, not just landscapes—the light need not come from only one point. Each element in a painting is shown as if lit from the point that will most enhance it, without reference to the other picture elements.

A landscape painting normally has three parts: foreground, middle ground, and distance. Sometimes these are not given equal value and occasionally the middle ground or the distance may become somewhat token; but all three are nearly always present in some degree. The foreground is at the bottom of the picture, with the middle ground above it and the distance above

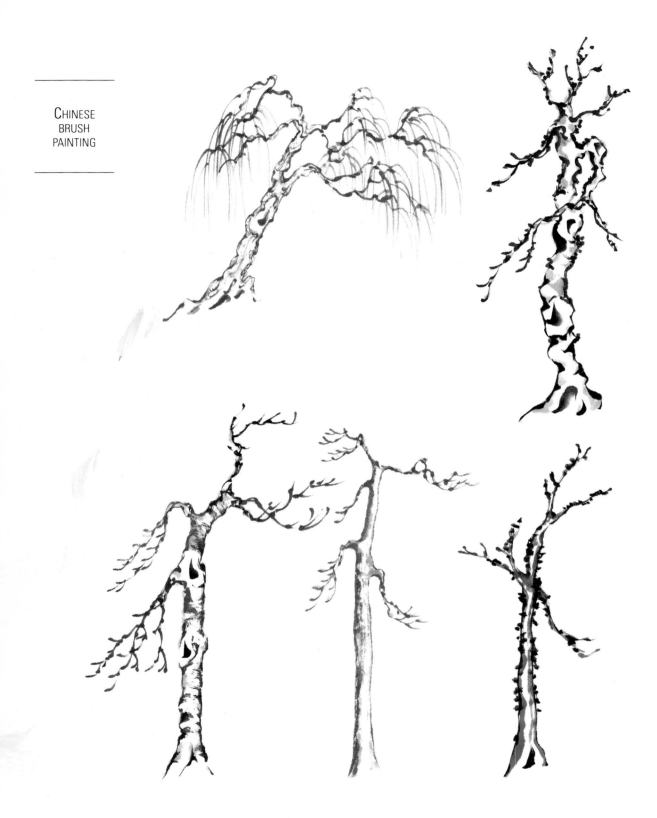

A selection of trees for landscape paintings.

that. You should always begin by painting the foreground and work upward. Traditionally, skies were left unpainted, as was water quite often, but today some artists treat the sky as their distance and depict it with ink and color.

When embarking on a landscape, you should start with a prominent feature of the foreground, such as a tree. Make this the reference point for your composition. Most Chinese landscapes contain evidence of man's presence—some houses, a boat, a figure or two—but this should not dominate the foreground. It is as if the artist is telling us of man's insignificant role in nature.

Traditionally, landscapes are first completed in ink tones and color is added later in light washes. Some schools of landscape painting use more definite colors, particularly greens and blues; these are also added to an ink painting.

Landscape elements

By now you will have mastered most of the techniques you need for painting landscapes. However, you also have to be able to portray the individual elements with which you can build your traditional Chinese landscape, and this section concentrates on these.

Illustrated opposite are examples of different kinds of trees. These are done in the same way as plum branches and pine trees, but the shapes and shading are adapted to suit the species. Different leaf patterns are shown below left, and below right are trees as they are depicted in the middle ground and distance. When coloring the foliage of bushes and trees, wet an area much larger than the one you want to color. Then add a wash, which should extend slightly outside the inked drawing to give a halo effect.

On page 108 is a selection of the kind of simple figures that frequently occur in Chi-

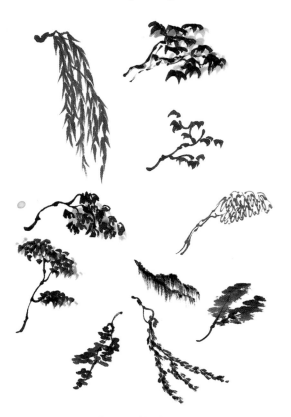

A selection of leaf patterns for landscape paintings.

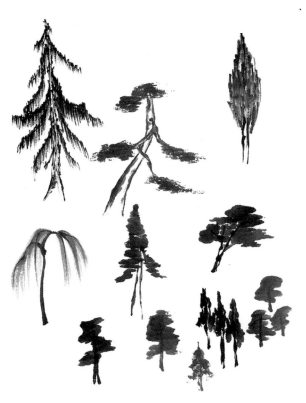

A selection of trees for the middle ground and distance in landscape paintings.

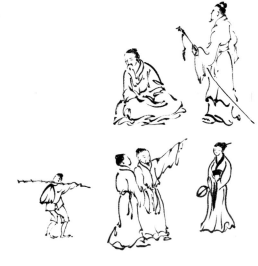

*Simple human figures suitable
for landscape paintings.*

nese landscape paintings. They are drawn with a fine-pointed brush, as are the boats shown below them. For the freestyle boat (below right), you should load your brush with two tones to paint the main shape with a single stroke. The sail is done by moving the brush, again loaded with two tones, from side to side. On the right are examples of buildings and bridges typical of those found in landscape paintings. When you color buildings, boats, people, and the trunks of trees, make sure they do not stand out too much from their surroundings.

Obviously, you may want to paint land-

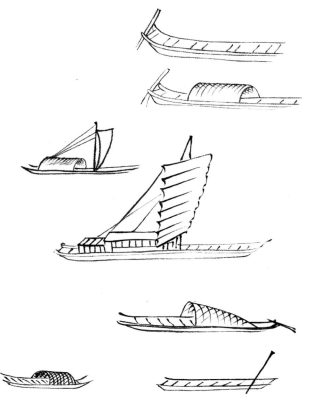

Boats typical of those found in landscape paintings.

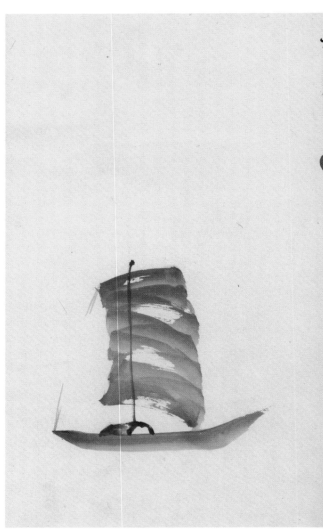

Freestyle boat.

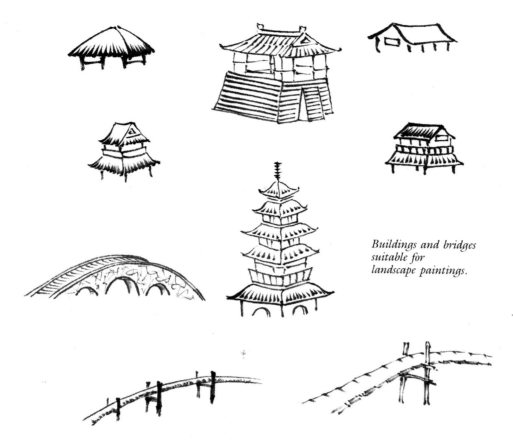

*Buildings and bridges
suitable for
landscape paintings.*

scapes that have Western boats, buildings, and people. You can easily do this, using the same techniques and simply adapting the shapes.

For rocks and mountains you should refer to the section on painting rocks (see page 52). Rocks in the middle ground are done in lighter tones than those in the foreground, and distant hills and mountains are done in very light tones. Some of the different brush strokes used to depict mountains and hills in landscape paintings are illustrated on the top of page 110. Sometimes, however, distant hills are shown very mistily by means of a washlike technique rather than by brush strokes. In **a** in the bottom illustration, for example, the hill has a clear outline but its base fades into the mist. To achieve this effect, wet a band of the paper just below where the ridge of your hill will come. Fill your largest brush with very watery ink and tip it in slightly darker ink. Using the tip to make the crest of the hill, roll the brush over the paper,

pressing the heel down into the damp portion of it. For a mountain totally shrouded in mist (as in **b**), wet the whole area so that the edge of your mountain bleeds into the sky area.

Color washes on mountains, land, and rocks are fairly self-explanatory. Foreground colors can be brighter than those in the middle ground, which in turn should be more dominant than those in the distance; but take care not to make your painting too garish. Be careful also to blend colors well; remember to use the heel of your brush. If you want to add snow-capped peaks to your distant mountains, wet the tops before you apply the color to the lower slopes and run the color into the wet portion to prevent a harsh edge. Similarly, misty areas at the bases of mountains and foothills should be dampened and have the wash run into them to avoid a watermark forming.

To suggest water, it is not necessary to use color. Still water is often left unpainted or with only a very light wash run into the

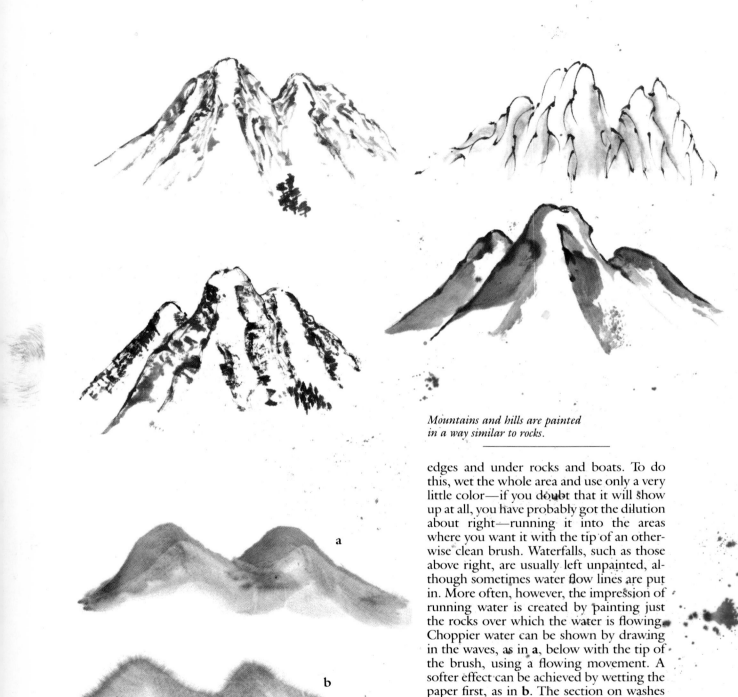

*Mountains and hills are painted
in a way similar to rocks.*

*Distant hills, showing
different misty effects.*

edges and under rocks and boats. To do this, wet the whole area and use only a very little color—if you doubt that it will show up at all, you have probably got the dilution about right—running it into the areas where you want it with the tip of an otherwise clean brush. Waterfalls, such as those above right, are usually left unpainted, although sometimes water flow lines are put in. More often, however, the impression of running water is created by painting just the rocks over which the water is flowing. Choppier water can be shown by drawing in the waves, as in **a**, below with the tip of the brush, using a flowing movement. A softer effect can be achieved by wetting the paper first, as in **b**. The section on washes (see page 115) will give you some more ideas for portraying water, as well as describing the general principles that are relevant when depicting still water.

For skies, too, you should consult the wash section. Be particularly careful not to make the color too heavy for skies. Remember that once a picture is mounted, the

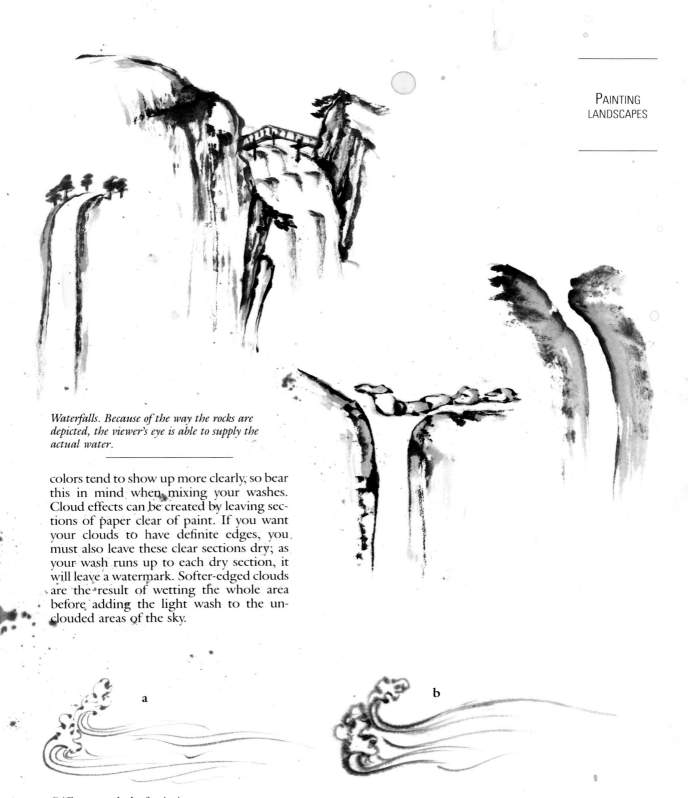

*Waterfalls. Because of the way the rocks are
depicted, the viewer's eye is able to supply the
actual water.*

colors tend to show up more clearly, so bear
this in mind when mixing your washes.
Cloud effects can be created by leaving sections of paper clear of paint. If you want
your clouds to have definite edges, you
must also leave these clear sections dry; as
your wash runs up to each dry section, it
will leave a watermark. Softer-edged clouds
are the result of wetting the whole area
before adding the light wash to the un-
clouded areas of the sky.

Different methods of painting waves.

111

Clouds with sharp edges are achieved by leaving areas of the paper dry so that the color wash creates watermarks when it encounters them.

The painting at right is a fairly formal typical Chinese landscape, whereas the painting on page 114 is done in a more freestyle manner. Both these paintings incorporate the elements describe earlier and are included here for you practice putting these elements together. For more experimental techniques in landscape painting, see page 119.

Once you have grasped the techniques of landscape painting, you will probably want to apply them to your own favorite scenery. You will find this easier to do if you happen to like painting mountains. Flat landscape can, of course, be depicted in the same three-tier perspective, but it looks somewhat strange to most Western eyes. If you are painting flat scenery, you will be well advised to experiment with perspective. A number of modern Chinese painters are departing from the rigid rules without undermining the Chinese character of their paintings. Many of them have adopted Western perspective while retaining the freshness of their approach, which enables them to use space as an expressive element in their continuing effort to capture the spirit of the scenery. The use of Western compositional techniques has not turned them into mere photographic recorders. You may well find some of the techniques discussed in the following chapters very useful when trying to convey the spirit of the landscape around you.

Landscape. *A typical formal landscape combining various landscape elements (private collection).*

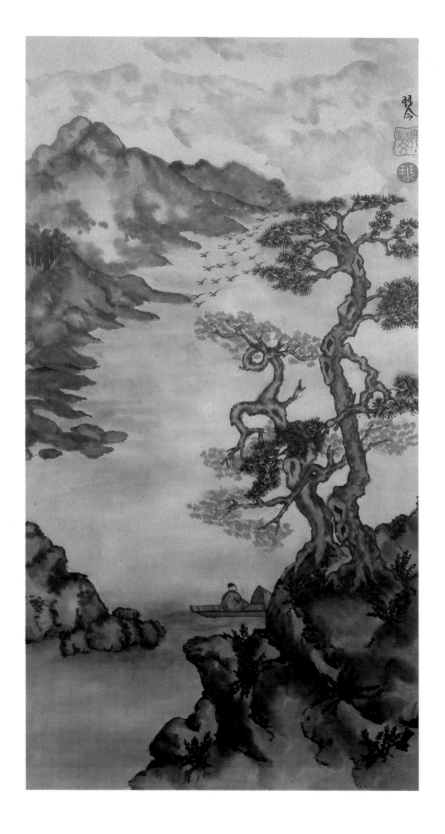

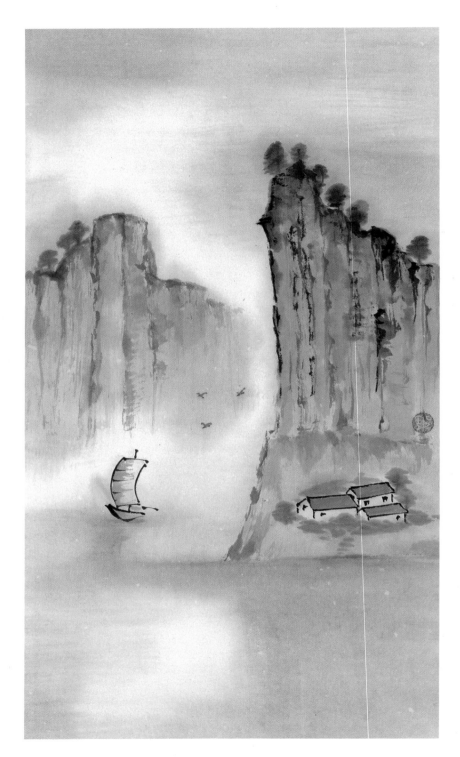

Landscape after Hau Chiok. *This freestyle painting follows traditional methods.*

APPLYING WASHES

Some styles of Chinese painting do not use washes at all; for example, Chan or Zen Buddhist paintings very seldom have washes. Many of your paintings, however, will be greatly enhanced by the addition of a wash, which can be an essential element of the composition.

There are a few basic rules that apply to any kind of wash. It is important that you always use a towel to lay your picture on before applying a wash. Newspaper can be used, but it tends to soak up moisture unevenly, resulting in a patchy effect. Be sure the towel you use still has some pile; a threadbare towel will leave a crisscross pattern on your painting. You must work with a proper wash brush (see page 22)—anything else will make life unnecessarily difficult. Always dampen your painting with clean water before applying any color since this will enable you to achieve an even spread of color. Do not swamp the picture with water; a light dampening is sufficient. Spread each brushload of color as far as it will go, varying the direction of your brush strokes, and make sure each new brushload overlaps a previous one so that you get an even blending. This is true even if your tones are changing and blending. Apply the wash over the subject rather than around it. Never hurry a wash.

If any wet spots appear where the paper has stuck to the towel, simply lift the paper gently and mop underneath with a tissue. This is important; otherwise the wash will dry spotty—but do remember how fragile the paper is when wet. If you find you are getting a great many spots, your paper must be too wet. Try gently mopping the whole painting with tissue. If this does not im-prove matters, your towel is probably unsuitable.

Some washes are applied to the front of a painting and some to the back. There is no fixed rule about this. If you want your colors to stand out clearly, you should put the wash on the back of the picture. If, however, you want to deaden a color slightly or create an underwater effect, you should apply the wash to the front. On a landscape you will almost certainly find it easier to work from the front.

The simplest wash is an evenly applied tea wash, as illustrated on page 37. Plum blossom pictures and simple studies of birds, insects, and flowers often have a tea wash. It gives a mellow, slightly antiqued effect. Use a ratio of six teabags to one cup of water. (Use Indian tea, not Chinese.) When the tea has thoroughly brewed, remove the teabags and leave the solution to cool. A tea wash is normally applied to the back of a painting.

Any even-toned wash is applied in the same way as a tea wash. If you are using color instead of tea, make the mixture very dilute. Take particular care if you are using blue for your wash because this color is often difficult to spread evenly and usually dries brighter than expected. Never try to mix ink with a wash as it tends to separate out from the color.

Often you will need a wash that is more than just an even-toned coloring of the paper. You may decide to concentrate the color behind a subject and fade it out toward the edges of the paper; you may want to have a variegated wash or leave some areas white (see page 85, right); you may need to suggest movement in water to de-

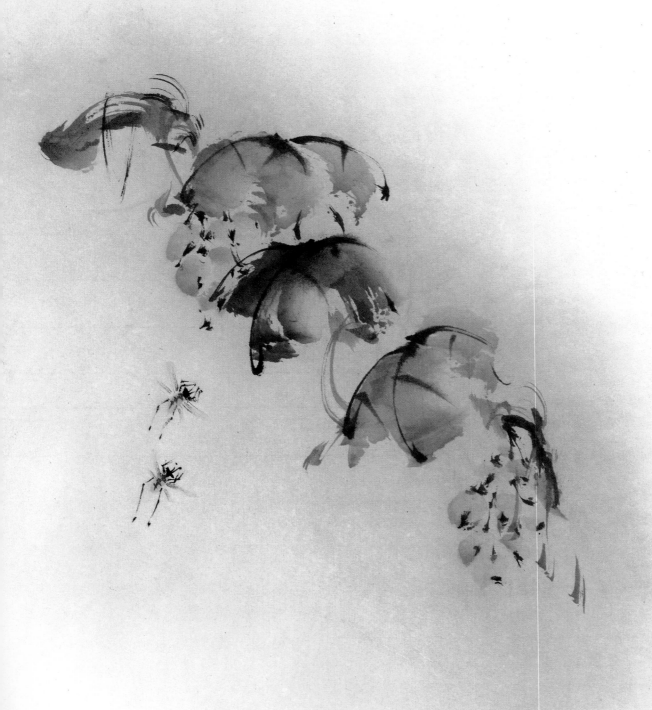

pict rain, shadows, or clouds; or you may want to make a rock look heavy and dense or a tree look leafy. You will be able to do all of these and more when you become skilled in the use of washes.

The technique is always essentially the same, and if you can manage to achieve an even-toned background wash, you should have no difficulty with the variations. The most important thing is to work slowly and carefully. Never panic. Remember that you can always add color but you cannot take it away, so be sparing with the colors when mixing them. Chinese colors are often very subtle and it is important to remember this when applying a wash. A color that hardly shows at all when the painting has dried will be surprisingly noticeable after you have mounted your painting. If you do put too much color on in one place, keep calm; the solution is to spread it as far as you can and then apply still more color to blend your overdarkened area into the rest of the wash and make the effect look deliberate.

Shown at left is an example of a wash where most of the color is concentrated behind the subject. It is done on the back of the painting. First of all, dampen the whole picture, then apply the first brushful of color to the center of the area where you want the wash to be concentrated and spread it outward from there, varying the angle of your brush and taking the color as far as it will go. If necessary, apply more color, making sure you overlap it with the already shaded area. You must spread the color to its fullest extent, even if it appears to be going into an area you want to leave unshaded. If you do not, you will not achieve a gradual fading out; rather, your wash will come to an abrupt stop.

Sometimes it is necessary to vary the colors in a wash. With a watery subject, such as the lotus on pages 67 and 70 or the fish on page 78, the wash can be a vital element in the composition. When you are using a wash in this way as an integral part of the picture, it is better to apply it to the front of your painting. The only time you might hesitate to do this is if you have some white

or very light colors in your painting that you wish to stand out; adding the wash to the front tends to dull white and colors mixed with white. The principles here are exactly the same as before, although you may with watery subjects want to use more definite colors than you would for a background wash. It is probably best to begin at the bottom of a painting with the darker tones and work upward to the lighter shades. Thus a lotus picture can have dark blues at the bottom, working up through varying shades of lighter blues and greens to light yellows and browns. Change the tones gradually and remember to take extra care to overlap your brush strokes so that there are no sudden color alterations. You can add some water swirls, as in the painting on page 78, with a large ordinary brush (not a wash brush). Load the brush with the wash tone and tip it with more concentrated color. Apply the brush to the paper so that both tones are used. This technique is similar to the one you used for the watery waves in the lesson on landscapes.

For some watery subjects you may prefer to use different depths of the same tone interspersed with areas of white paper. This was the case for the fish on page 81. The method here is slightly different because you want to suggest water movement, so you should keep your brush strokes working in one direction, that is, horizontally. Leave parts of the paper white and add some dark streaks of the same color as your wash. As before, you can add movement to your water, as on page 102, by means of the technique for waves.

The background to the picture of mandarin ducks on page 90 makes use of a very similar technique. The whole painting was dampened and then the water wash applied to the blue area. The shore line was emphasized with an ordinary-shaped brush and the color then blended into the blue area with a clean wash brush. This results in the uncolored area looking snowy.

Remember that watery pictures can often be enhanced by adding reeds and lily pads before the wash has dried.

Landscapes often feature areas of still water and, as suggested in the chapter on landscapes, it can be effective to leave these unpainted. Introduce shading just around

The wash in this painting is concentrated behind the image.

the edge and under any boats and rocks. It is not necessary to dampen the whole painting, but you will need to wet all the water area, not just the places where you intend to add color. You can give water in landscapes a more comprehensive coloring if you want to, in which case use the techniques described above for waterlike washes. Again, you need only dampen the area that represents water before you apply the wash.

Rocks and mountains in landscape paintings are often colored just by means of a wash. Remember to make the foreground tones darker and richer than those in the middle and far distance, and take care not to make the rocks too multicolored or bright. However, you should vary the tones somewhat, especially in the foreground. You will also find that trees can often be enhanced by the addition of a soft wash over the leaf area. This gives the foliage a denser look and adds a slight halo effect to the trees. Make sure you dampen an area that is larger than the one you want to color and do not forget to fade out the shading as you did for the illustration on page 116. All these techniques are illustrated on page 113.

As already mentioned, skies are often left white or given a light, even-toned wash. You can also blend the tones in the sky as you did for water, but using more diluted color. Other techniques are possible, too. You can have a darker area of sky at hilltop level perhaps, lightening further up; or you can have a darker area at the top of your painting with a lighter tone behind the mountains, say, and maybe a hint of yellow to suggest sunshine (see the illustrations on pages 120 to 122, which illustrate some of the effects that can be achieved). Clouds can be depicted as described in the chapter on landscapes, or you can superimpose them on your wash in a manner similar to that used to convey water movement. Add darker or lighter tone in a cloudlike shape with a large soft brush and blend it in carefully with your wash brush (see the paintings on pages 124, left, and 125).

Experiment with washes. Chinese paper is amazingly strong and adaptable, and if you remember that it is more fragile when wet, you should be able to create some exciting effects. In the next chapter you will see that by experimenting with textures and colors you can execute paintings that consist almost entirely of washes.

MORE ADVENTUROUS TECHNIQUES

By now you will have long since discovered how versatile Chinese paper, ink, color, and brushes are. You should have mastered their use sufficiently to be able to treat them a little less reverently. You may also be growing a little frustrated by the limitations of traditional Chinese painting: its formality, its stylization of scenery, its strange (to Western eyes) perspective, its "foreignness." You may in fact be wondering if Chinese brush painting can be made more responsive to the "needs" of the Western eye. If so, you are ready to branch out and do your own thing; to find your own subjects and experiment with your materials and techniques. An excellent book to give you some ideas for new approaches is *Oriental Watercolor Techniques* by Frederick Wong (Watson-Guptill, 1977).

You may also find that you want to depict particular scenes rather than landscape in general. Although this may be a departure from the traditional Chinese approach to landscape painting, it is only partly so. For practical reasons you cannot sit in front of a scene and paint it unless you are prepared to go to a great deal of trouble with tables and paperweights, so actually you will be painting remembered places (although you may want to aid your memory with photographs). All the paintings illustrated in this chapter are of actual places but remain true to the Chinese principle of capturing their spirit. In fact, they reflect what many Chinese painters both in and out of China have tried to do in the past to evolve techniques that provide extra dimensions for the medium. Recently there has probably been

more experimentation than ever before, largely because Western ideas have introduced into China a fervor for "originality."

Most of the techniques described in this chapter rely on the strength of the paper, and you should therefore only try them with good-quality paper. The cheap rolls of very white paper tend to disintegrate when wet, and nearly every variation here requires the paper to be worked damp. The first examples particularly need good paper because the technique requires it to be crumpled when wet and later stretched flat again for mounting.

To achieve the textured effect of the landscape, on pages 120 and 121, first dampen your paper evenly with a wash brush and then crumple it into a tight ball. Very carefully unwad it and lay it out on your piece of old towel. Fill a large brush with light ink and skim over the areas where you want shading. Put in some darker tones in the same way. Again using the skimming method, add some light colors. Let the paper partly dry and add some more strokes; these will not soak in as much as the previous ones and should be in slightly more definite tones. When the paper has completely dried, put in more texture in the same way, using dark ink and colors. You may find you need to recrumple the paper before you do this because your previous steps will have tended to flatten it. Once these latest strokes are dry, however, the paper needs to be flat again, so redampen it to achieve this. While it is wet, add the washes for the water and the sky, then leave it to dry and put in details in the normal

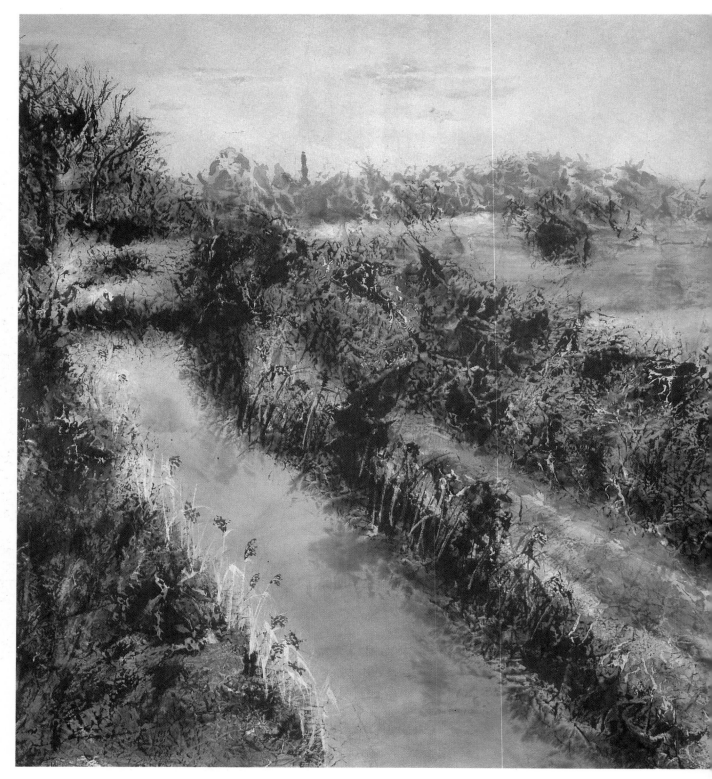

120

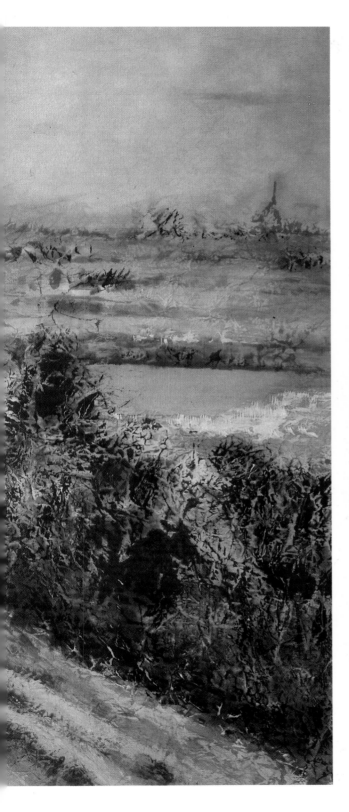

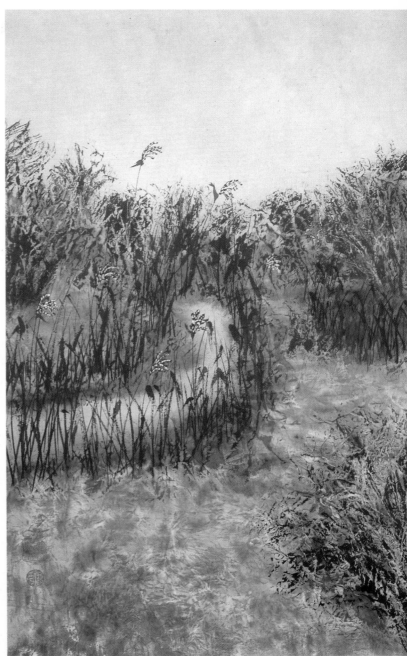

Wicken Fen, Cambridgeshire. *The crumpled
paper technique is used here, but the perspective is
entirely Western.*

View from Wicken Fen. *The crumpled paper
technique is also used for the picture shown left.
The perspective, however, is typical of a Chinese
brush painting (private collection).*

121

way. Do not worry about the slightly crumpled appearance of your picture at this stage; it will look fine after it has been mounted. Traditionally, this creased paper technique has been used to depict mountains, but as you can see from the illustrations here, it is equally effective when used to represent dry vegetation.

The painting was built up from the foreground in the traditional way and includes the three elements of foreground, middle ground, and distance. The next painting (page 121, right) was done by exactly the same technique, but without the Chinese perspective. The distance is provided by the sky, but the focus is on the middle ground, which was therefore the starting point for the picture. This also applies to the painting shown below, although this time appropriately snowy tones were used for the wet

Wicken Fen in the Snow. *An additional snowy effect is added with a fine spray of white gouache.*

Morning Mist in Bornea (*private collection*).

texturing and thick white in place of strong black for the ground. An extra powdery effect was achieved by adding a very light dusting of white. The best way to do this is by spraying paint from a toothbrush with the back of a knife. Practice first, however, because directing the spray can be tricky.

A number of interesting effects can be achieved by applying the paint with materials other than paint brushes—for example, tissue, silk, a sponge, or a toothbrush. In the painting at right most of the color was applied with a sponge. The paper was dampened as if for a wash and the dark shapes were mapped in with light ink and a sponge, beginning with the trees in the foreground. The mountains were painted in the normal way with a brush. Once the picture had dried, darker tones were added to the trees, followed by light green tones also applied with a sponge. The details of

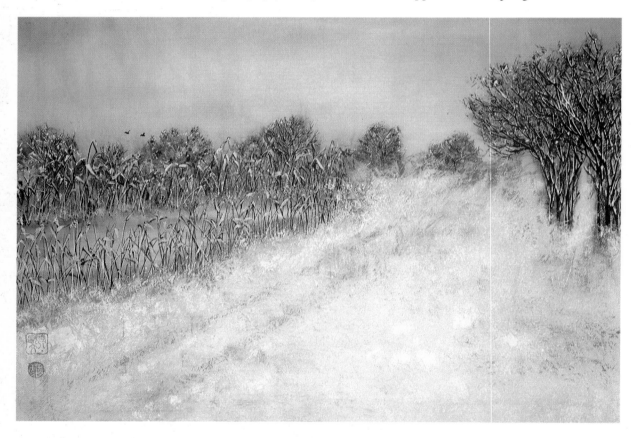

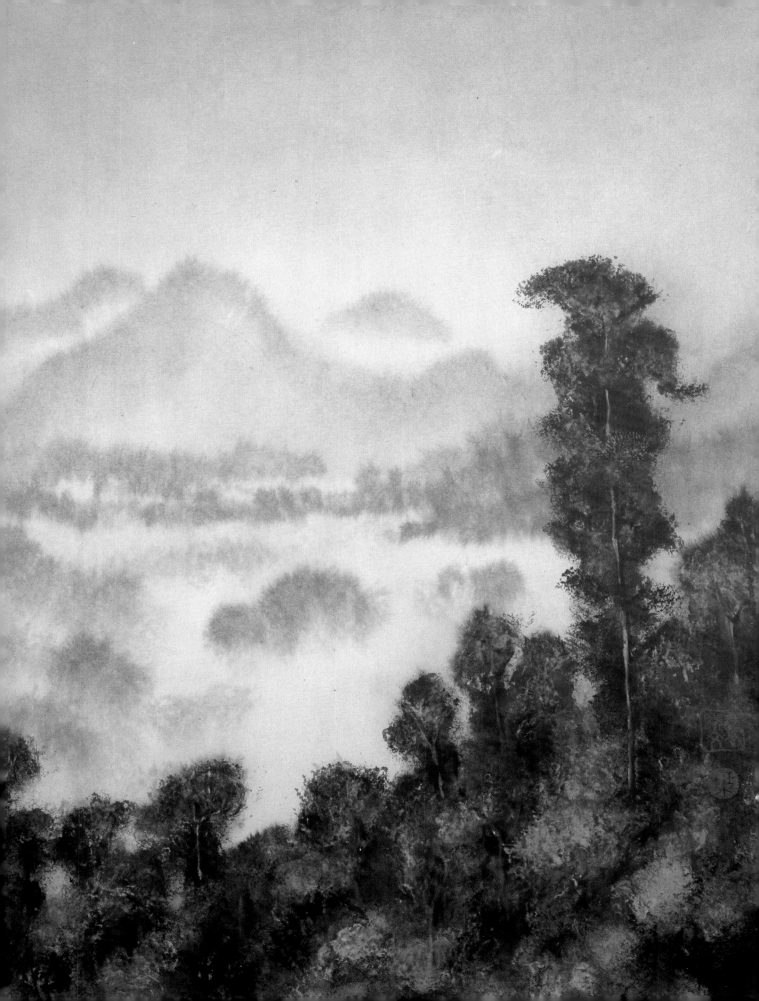

the trees were put in with a brush and a light wash added to the mountains and distant bushes. A wash was applied for the sky and mist.

The same technique was used for the picture of Ely Cathedral below. The cathedral itself was drawn in with a small brush while the paper was still wet. A few details were added after the paper had dried. The sky was done using the techniques described in the chapter on landscapes (see page 111). Most of the painting shown above, by contrast, was done in the style of a conventional Chinese landscape, although for the trees in the foreground a sponge was used.

Skies are particularly fascinating and can be the most dramatic element in a land-

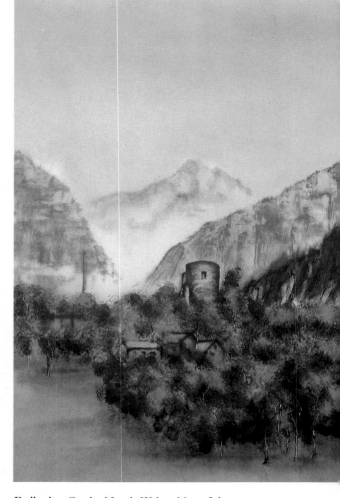

Dolbadan Castle, North Wales. *Most of the techniques used in this picture are traditional, although the trees in the foreground are done with a sponge. The perspective is Western, but there is a very clear distinction between foreground, middle ground, and distance.*

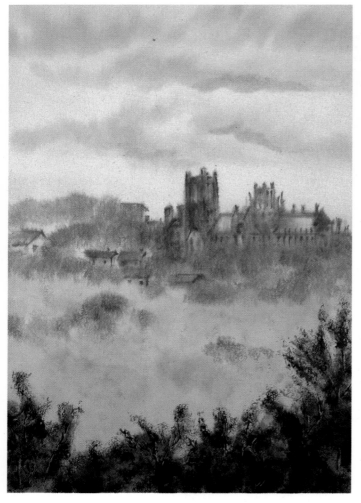

Ely Cathedral. *This painting is done with a combination of brush and sponge.*

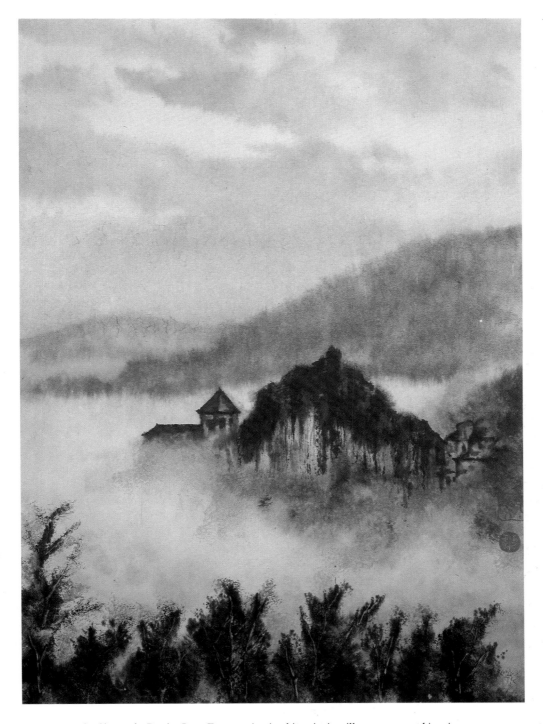

St Cirque-la-Popie, Lot, France. *Again this painting illustrates a combination
of traditional and experimental techniques. There is a clear foreground,
middle ground, and distance, and the clouds and distant hills are done
traditionally; but the trees in the foreground are done with
a sponge and so are the mist effects, on dampened paper.*

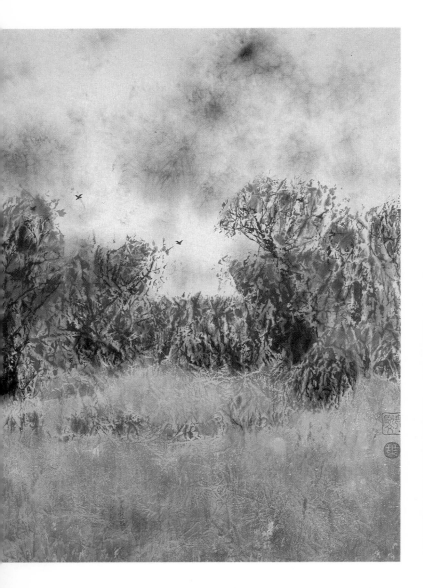

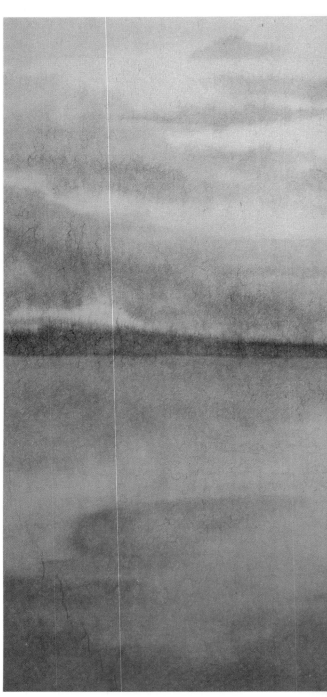

Wandlebury, Cambridgeshire. *The unusual technique used to create the sky in this painting produces an interesting and effective result.*

---

scape. Although by being fairly adventurous with color quite spectacular results can be achieved with traditional Chinese methodology (see page 125), it is fun to experiment with different effects and methods. For example, the painting above shows an interesting sky effect. To achieve this, wet the paper, wad it into a ball, and place it in a shallow pool of very diluted wash color. Remove the paper from the color and turn

The Mekong River. *The entire painting really consists of a wash (private collection).*

126

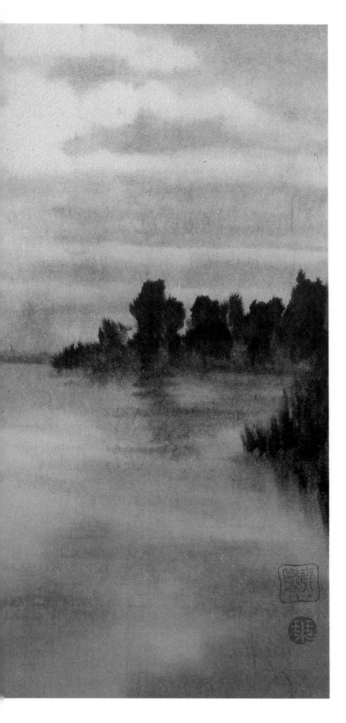

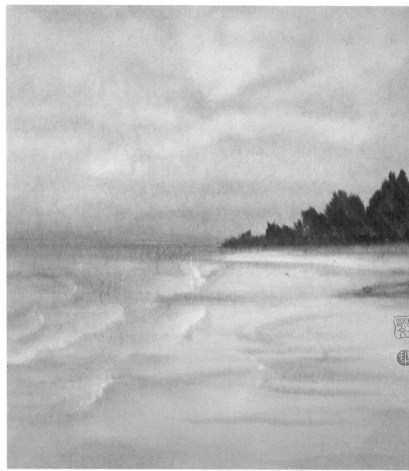

Diani Beach, Kenya. *Untypically, white is added to the wash color to help make the sky look threatening and to depict the waves running onto the beach.*

the still-wadded-up ball upside down. Leave it for a few moments to allow some of the color to seep down. Then uncrumple the ball very carefully. The vegetation in the same picture was done by the crumpled paper technique used for the paintings on pages 120 and 122. A powdery yellow was added by means of the toothbrush technique to give the grass in the foreground a polleny look.

In the paintings at left, above, and on page 128, all the paint was applied with a very large soft brush. At left and above, the whole painting was executed on wet paper. For Diani Beach, a light color wash was

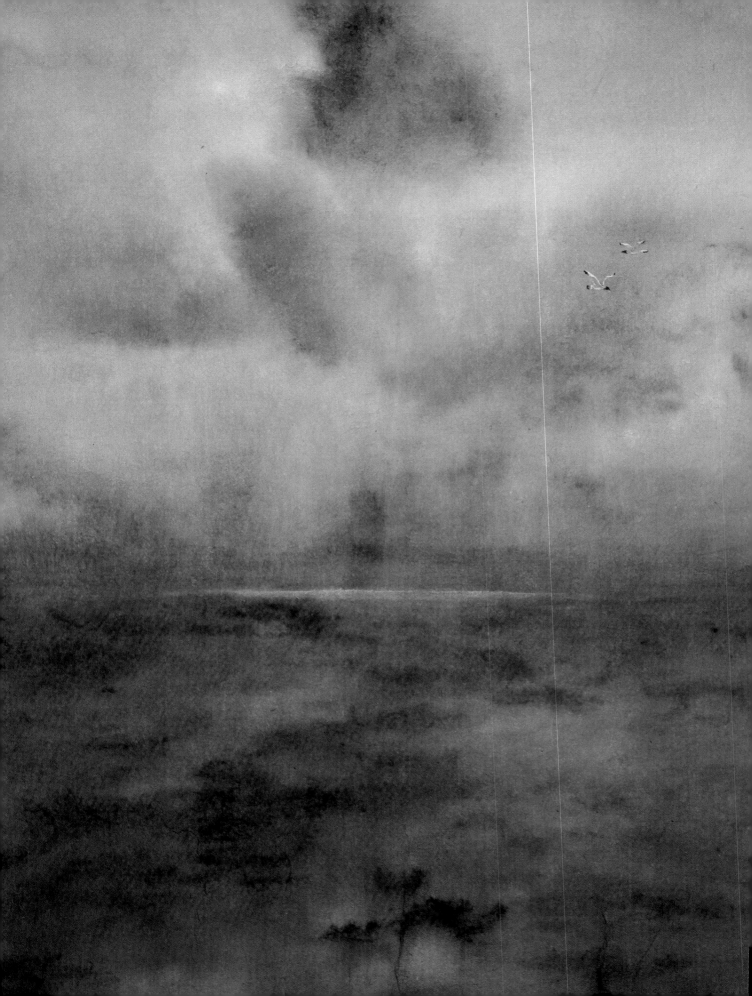

Storm Brewing in the Channel. *The entire painting is really a wash, although texture is added to the water with a dry brush.*

applied and then streaks of darker tone added (as for the waves described in the chapter on washes), which resulted in a wet-looking beach. White was used to make the clouds and mixed with ink for the darker sections to give them substance. For the illustration of Diani Beach on page 13, the boat and the man were outlined on dry paper. Then the paper was dampened and the sky and water put in, using wash techniques but thickening some of the colors with white. After the paper had dried, detail was added to the boat and figure.

The painting at left was done in a similar way. In this instance there was no focal point like a shoreline or trees, so the sky and sea were done first. Some of the clouds were added very wet and were not blended in, so they ran erratically into the previously applied wash, creating a watery effect. After

the basic blended wash had started to dry, the sea was textured with a dry brush. The light rays were added with carefully directed strokes of a wash brush when the painting was nearly dry. The birds were added last.

The same technique used to suggest the sun's rays, described above, can also be used to create an effect of rain. The painting below shows how falling rain can be suggested by raking the picture with strokes from a wide wash brush. Rain and snow effects can also be created by splashing dirty water or white paint in small droplets as in the illustration on page 17, although the lying snow here was placed in spots where it would be likely to collect. The wash was applied to the back of the painting.

As you can see, you will usually find that you need to employ a combination of tech-

Rainy Scene in Norfolk. *The rain effect is created with carefully directed strokes of a wash brush.*

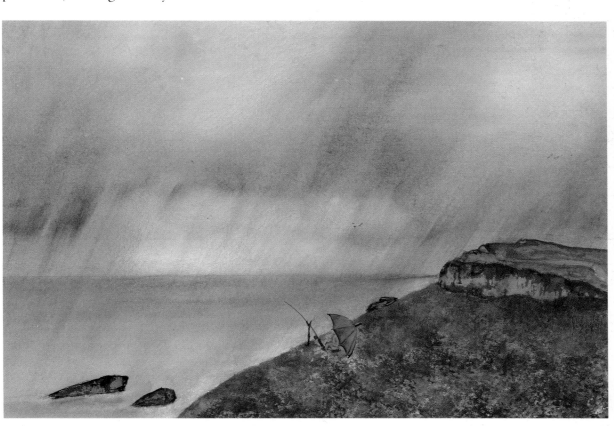

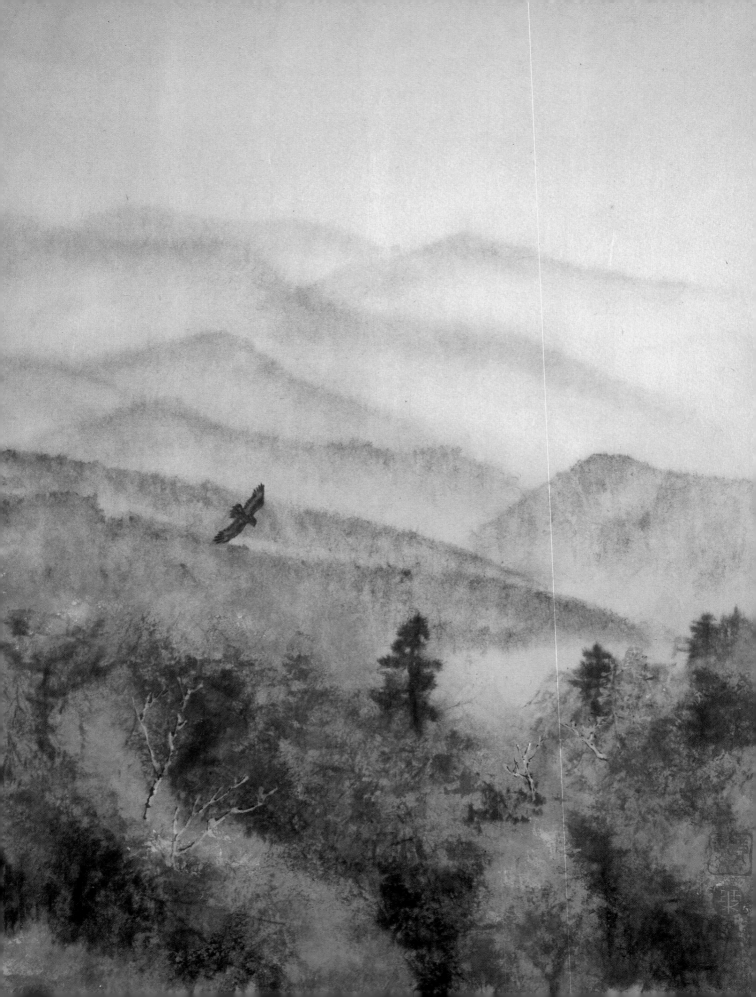

niques to create the effect you desire. For example, in the painting at left, the vegetation in the foreground was done by using the crumpled paper technique; the middle-distance hills were put in with a sponge to create a wooded effect; and the distant hills were painted with a brush on wet paper. In the illustration on page 136 the cliffs were painted by using the side of a dry brush; the vegetation was added with a sponge; and the water was applied with a wash in the normal way.

If you want to experiment further, you can also make interesting pictures by using materials other than Chinese paper to paint on. Watercolor paper is nonabsorbent and can create various effects, provided you remember not to try adding a wash. Silk is, of course, a traditional painting material; Chinese picture silk is sized with alum, but you can also work on unsized silk. The fabric used for screen printing is another possibility. Any fine woven fabric, even some synthetics, should take Chinese inks well.

The Smokey Mountains. *A combination of different techniques using brush, sponge, and crumpled paper is used in this painting (private collection).*

MOUNTING AND PRESENTATION

By the time you have finished a painting, especially if you have given it a wash or used the crumpled paper technique, it will probably look somewhat the worse for wear. You now need to back your painting in order to flatten and stretch it. Even if the paper is still in pristine condition, the picture should be mounted to give it durability.

Paper
Ideally you should use the paper made specifically for backing pictures, but it is not generally available in the United States. You can, however, find reasonable substitutes. Good-quality *shuan* paper is suitable because it tends to stretch at the same rate as the painting and therefore does not pull against it. Unfortunately it is rather expensive to use as backing and it leaves you with a somewhat flimsy end product that tends to wrinkle when it is framed. If you do use it, remember that *shuan* paper is fragile when wet and be very careful as you smooth it on the painting; otherwise you may end up with holes in your painting.

You can also back paintings with good-quality watercolor paper, which works well. The *shuan* paper takes to it fairly readily and the result is flat and even. For very large paintings, watercolor paper is often the best solution since it can be bought in various sizes up to double elephant (40 × 60 inches). The disadvantages, though, are that it is very expensive and it can impart a slightly heavy effect to the painting.

The most satisfactory substitute that I have found is heavy-duty wallpaper or un-coated shelf-lining paper. It stretches in harmony with the *shuan* paper and absorbs the glue well. It is cheap and easy to find in houseware and hardware stores. Its only real drawback is that it only comes in standard-width rolls and is therefore unusable for large paintings. You must use heavy, uncoated, shelf paper; the lighter-weight ones tend to wrinkle badly.

Newsprint is unsuitable for mounting Chinese brush paintings because it can result in air bubbles and wrinkles.

Glue
Use commercial wallpaper paste. When you buy paste, make sure you get an old-fashioned wheat-based one. The best kind is paste for lightweight wallpapers. Avoid pastes that are based on synthetic compounds because they are too powerful and can cause your painting to disintegrate.

You will also need a mounting brush (see page 23). These are readily available in most Chinese stores or you can use a good-quality 1½-inch bristle brush. An ordinary household paint brush can also be used. The bristles must not be too stiff, however, and you should take extra care with it because it will be rougher on the *shuan* paper than a proper Chinese mounting brush.

Mounting technique
You should work on a surface that can be cleaned easily. A Formica table top is the most suitable working surface for mounting paintings.

Before you begin gluing your painting,

cut a piece of backing paper that is at least 2 inches larger all around than the painting. Place this within easy reach. Put the painting face down on the working surface and brush the glue all over the back until the whole painting is soaked. As you apply the glue, try to eliminate the air between the table top and the painting. This is easiest to do if you begin applying the glue in the center and work outward. If the paper becomes strained at any point, work an adjoining area to ease it. Try to avoid creases, although any that do occur can usually be worked gently outward. Do not hurry and, above all, do not get overanxious; the glue will not dry even if it takes a while to work out air bubbles and creases.

When the whole painting is soaked with glue and there is no air trapped between it and the table top, wipe up the glue that has spread on the table and make sure that the area surrounding the picture is clean and dry. Place the center of the backing paper on the center of the back of the painting. Smooth the backing onto the back of the painting by working outward from the middle. When you are satisfied that the backing is properly glued and there are no air bubbles, peel the paper carefully off the table and the painting will come with it.

To ensure that the painting dries as flat as possible, place it face up and apply paste to the area of backing paper around the edge of the painting. Then lift the backed painting carefully off the table, place it face first on a smooth, vertical wall, and stick the margin down. Create an air cushion between the wall and the painting by pushing a small straw through and blowing some air in between the wall and the picture (see below). After the painting has dried, peel it off the wall.

You may not, however, have a wall that you wish to cover with old glue stains, and this much fuss is not really necessary if you are using the heavier weights of paper as recommended. It is a lot simpler to lay your painting face up on a clean, dry, flat surface and carefully weight the margin all the way around. When the painting is dry, trim off the margins and you should have no trouble getting your picture to lie flat in a frame.

Problems with backing paintings are almost always caused by using the wrong equipment or materials. Make sure that you have the correct paper for backing; it must be soft, fibrous, and fairly thick. Paper that is too thin or nonabsorbent will wrinkle badly when it comes into contact with the glued painting. Your glue must not only be the right kind, but must also be the right consistency. If it is too watery, it will not be sticky enough; if it is too thick, it will not spread evenly and will tend to be lumpy.

Any other problems you encounter with mounting will probably be the result of carelessness. As when applying a wash, you must not hurry the process. Because *shuan* paper is so fragile when it is wet, too heavy a hand may result in holes in your painting. Be patient if you have an air bubble or wrinkle that is more recalcitrant than usual; just work it gently out. Large or very long paintings need extra care because the *shuan* paper will not always stretch evenly. Sometimes it is better to settle for a small crease

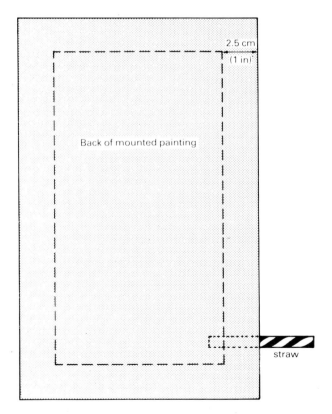

The traditional method of drying a mounted painting.

rather than risk a tear. After you become skilled at mounting, you should be able to repair tears in a painting with patience and care.

Presentation

Ideally, a Chinese brush painting should be mounted on a scroll with a silk surround. This is a process that requires skill and is governed by a great many rules and much tradition. For example, monochrome paintings and those with delicate color should have a light-colored silk surround; dark-colored silk should only be used for remounting Song and Yuan paintings; and elaborate paintings with lots of gold, blue, and yellow in them should traditionally be mounted with a three-color surround. There are even rules of taste governing the material for the end pieces of the scroll—the most desirable being made of black sandalwood.

Unfortunately, there is nobody in the United States who can scroll paintings properly. Amateurish efforts to create scrolls always look just that—amateurish. If you cannot send your paintings to Hong Kong to be done properly, then it is better to frame them.

Obviously, the way you frame your pictures is largely a matter of personal taste, but some general observations may be helpful. Chinese brush paintings look best in simple frames with light-colored mats. Framing shops are often eager to suggest mock bamboo moldings but they somewhat belabor the point. Large landscape paintings seem to be able to take a Western-style mat cut in the usual way, with the bottom slightly deeper than the top and sides, and placed on top of the painting. Very conventional landscapes and simpler subjects seem to benefit from a compromise between the constraints imposed by a Western frame and the balance of a Chinese scroll. Traditionally the widest band of the silk surround is above the painting, the one beneath it being about two-thirds as wide and the side bands narrow. The largest band is sometimes thought to represent heaven and the lower one earth; these two are occasionally referred to as the jade pools. If you do want to put a Chinese-style surround on your painting before you frame it, you can

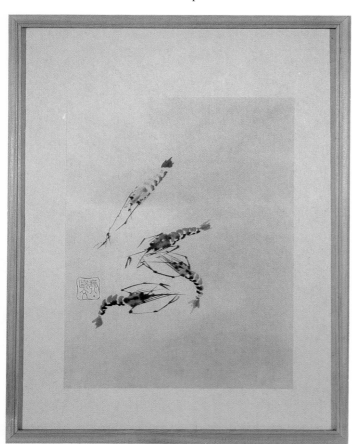

Prawns. *This painting is done in the style of Qi Baishi. Although framed in a conventional Western molding, the simplicity of the Chinese-style composition is emphasized by the proportions of the mount. The painting is laid on top of a faintly figured Japanese paper, with the deepest section above the picture.*

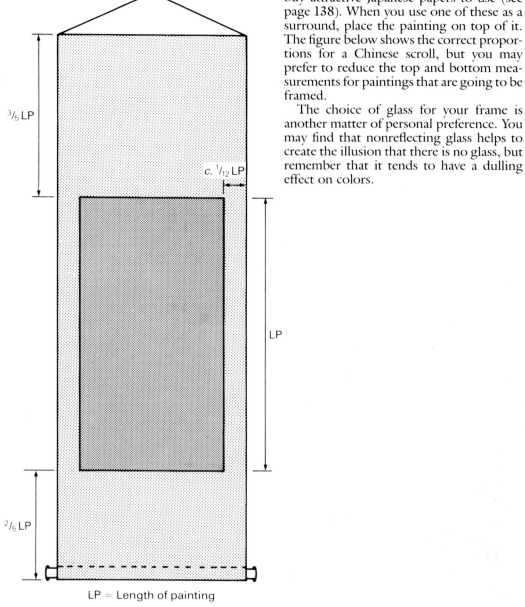

$^3/_5$ LP

c. $^1/_{12}$ LP

LP

$^2/_5$ LP

LP = Length of painting

The correct proportions for a Chinese painting hung on a scroll.

buy attractive Japanese papers to use (see page 138). When you use one of these as a surround, place the painting on top of it. The figure below shows the correct proportions for a Chinese scroll, but you may prefer to reduce the top and bottom measurements for paintings that are going to be framed.

The choice of glass for your frame is another matter of personal preference. You may find that nonreflecting glass helps to create the illusion that there is no glass, but remember that it tends to have a dulling effect on colors.

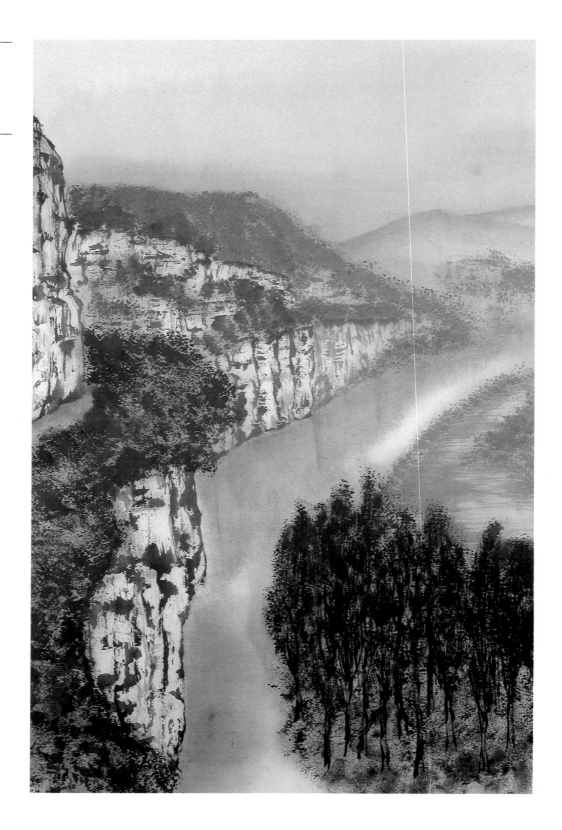

)N CONCLUSION

By now you have probably decided what kind of Chinese brush painting you most enjoy doing and looking at. Try to see as many original paintings as possible, in addition to looking at reproductions in books. A number of museums have good collections of Chinese paintings, and there are increasing numbers of exhibitions of modern works. Looking at actual paintings rather than reproductions is helpful in giving you a better idea of scale. Chinese paintings are usually rather large, which may come as a surprise. Because you will be able to see the mount as well, you will get a much clearer idea of proportions, since the way a painting is mounted is often very important to the overall impact it makes. Mounts are seldom included in reproductions of paintings in books. Also, of course,

books often illustrate only a detail from a painting and not the whole thing. This is particularly regrettable in the case of Chinese paintings, where space is such an important element of the composition.

Even though it is important to have followed the whole course of lessons here in sequence, there is no reason why you should not now decide to concentrate on or specialize in one or two subjects that you particularly enjoy. You may want to paint nothing but birds and flowers or perhaps traditional landscapes. You may choose to leave traditional styles alone and experiment with newer techniques. Whatever you decide, try to paint from your own experience and to develop an individual style while remembering the rules and precepts of Chinese painting.

The River Célé, Lot, France. *There is no need to feel that your paintings must use only traditional or only experimental techniques. By all means combine them as much as you like, as has been done in this painting.*

137

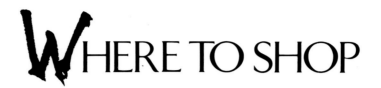

WHERE TO SHOP

Materials and equipment

More and more art-supply stores are selling materials for Chinese brush painting. Most good shops also have Japanese Teppachi colors and good-quality hake wash brushes. You should avoid, however, expensive kits containing brushes, ink stone, and ink stick—the brushes are usually poor, and you will pay more than usual for the stone and stick.

If your local art-supply store does not carry Chinese painting materials and cannot order them, you can order from the following companies by mail.

Daniel Smith Inc.
4130 First Avenue S.
Seattle, WA 98134
(206) 223-9599

Arthur Brown & Brothers
2 West 46th Street
New York, NY 10036
(212) 575-5555

Both of these are large mail-order companies that sell a wide range of artists' supplies, including Chinese painting materials. Since each offers different things, you might get both catalogs.

Unique Artists Supply Co.
444 Grand Avenue
San Francisco, CA 94108
(415) 986-1822

In addition to other supplies, also offers chops (seals).

Jub Tai Cheoon,
274 Queens Road C,
Hong Kong

Man Lune Choon,
29-35 Wing Kut Street,
Harvest Building,
2nd Floor, Flat B,
Hong Kong

Both of these shops specialize in art supplies and carry a very wide range of brushes, inks, colors, paper, silk, fan bases, chops, books, and anything else you could possibly want. They will ship items to the United States, but you will need to write first for a catalog and price list, since goods have to be paid for in advance.

Where to look at paintings

Most major museums in the United States and Canada have oriental painting collections. A visit to them will give you a much better understanding of Chinese brush painting techniques. The following lists some of the more outstanding or extensive collections. Those marked by an asterisk (*) are exclusively collections of Asian art.

*Asian Art Museum, San Francisco, California
*Asia Society Galleries, New York, New York
Cleveland Museum of Art, Cleveland, Ohio
Freer Gallery of Art, Smithsonian Institution, Washington, D.C.
Honolulu Academy of Arts, Honolulu, Hawaii
Los Angeles County Museum of Art, Los Angeles, California
Metropolitan Museum of Art, New York, New York
Minnesota Institute of Art, Minneapolis, Minnesota
Museum of Fine Arts, Boston, Massachusetts
*Nelson-Atkins Museum of Fine Art, Kansas City, Missouri
National Gallery of Canada, Ottawa, Ontario
*Oriental Institute, Chicago, Illinois
*Pacific Asia Museum, Pasadena, California
Portland Art Museum, Portland, Oregon
Royal Ontario Museum, Toronto, Canada
Seattle Art Museum, Seattle, Washington

If you are fortunate enough to visit the Far East, be sure to see the following collections of Chinese painting.

Cheng Te-Kun Collection, Hong Kong
Daitoku-ji, Kyoto, Japan
National Palace Museum, Taibei (Taiwan)
Palace Museum, Beijing
Shanghai Museum, Shanghai
Tokyo National Museum, Tokyo, Japan

BIBLIOGRAPHY

I have not attempted to provide an exhaustive list of books about Chinese and Japanese painting here, including only those of which I have some personal knowledge. The first section contains details of books that I have found especially interesting or useful. In the second section I have listed a wider selection of works.

Au Ho-nien, *Ink and Colour Paintings of Au Ho-nien*, Art Book Co., Ltd, Taipei, 1984. A collection of works by one of the modern exponents of the Lingnam school.

Chen Shuren, *The Art of Chen Shuren*, Urban Council of Hong Kong, 1980. A biography of one of the founders of the Lingnam school, including examples of his works.

Gao Jianfu, *The Art of Gao Jianfu*, Urban Council of Hong Kong, 1981. A biography of the founding father of the Lingnam school, including examples of his works.

Gao Qifeng, *The Art of Gao Qifeng*, Urban Council of Hong Kong, 1981. A biography of one of the founders of the Lingnam school, including examples of his works.

Hua Junwu (ed.), *Contemporary Chinese Painting*, New World Press, Beijing, 1983. A selection of works by most of the important painters in China at present, together with essays about Chinese brush painting by leading Chinese authorities on the subject.

Kwo Da-Wei, *Chinese Brushwork—Its History, Aesthetics and Techniques*, Allanheld & Schram, Monclair, 1981, and George Prior, London, 1981. The sections on history and esthetics provide a thorough discussion of the development and philosophy of Chinese brush painting and a clear explanation of the esthetics.

Lim, Lucy (organizer), *Contemporary Chinese Painting—An Exhibition from the People's Republic of China*, The Chinese Culture Foundation of San Francisco, 1983. This exhibition catalog contains examples of and interesting essays about contemporary Chinese painting by James Cahill, Michael Sullivan, Lucy Lim, and other Chinese artists and critics.

Moss, Hugh, *Some Recent Developments in Twentieth Century Chinese Painting: A Personal View*, Umbrella, Hong Kong, 1982. Hugh Moss concentrates on the developments in Chinese painting that have taken place outside China.

Rodzinski, Witold, *The Walled Kingdom: A History of China from 2000 BC to the Present*, Fontana, London, 1984. A very readable history of China which puts the development of its art into the context of its general history.

Sullivan, Michael, *The Arts of China*, University of California Press, Berkeley, 1967 (reprinted 1984). A history of Chinese art that puts painting in its wider context.

Symbols of Eternity—The Art of Landscape Painting in China, Clarendon Press, Oxford, 1979. A history of landscape painting and its philosophy.

Sze Mai-Mai (ed.), *The Mustard Seed Garden Manual of Painting*, Princeton University Press, Princeton, New Jersey, 1977. The easiest to come by of the classic Chinese texts on painting methods.

Wong, Frederick, *Oriental Watercolor Techniques*, Watson-Guptill Publications, New York, 1977. Although Frederick Wong is not strictly a Chinese brush painter, he provides a lot of ideas for interesting ways of using Chinese paper, ink, and colors.

Addis, Stephen, *Nanga Paintings*, Robert G. Sawers, London, 1975

Awakawa, Yasuichi, *Zen Painting*, translated by John Bester, Kodansha International, Ltd, Tokyo, New York and San Francisco, 1970

Bancroft, Anne, *Zen—Direct Pointing to Reality*, Thames & Hudson, London, 1979

Barnet, Sylvan & Burto, William, *Zen Ink Paintings*, Robert G. Sawers, London, with the cooperation of Kodansha International, Ltd, 1982

Binyon, Laurence, *Painting in the Far East—An Introduction to the History of Pictorial Art in Asia, Especially in China and Japan*, Dover Publications, Inc., New York, 1969

Cahill, James, *Chinese Painting*, Skira, Geneva, 1977, and Macmillan London, Ltd, London and Basingstoke, 1977

Capon, Edmund, *Chinese Painting*, Phaidon Press, Ltd, Oxford, 1979

Clayre, Alasdair, *The Heart of the Dragon*, Collins/Harvill, London, 1984

Fang Zhaoling, *Painting and Calligraphy*, Fang Zhaoling, Hong Kong, 1981

Frunzetti, Ion, *Classical Chinese Painting* (original title: *The Spirit of Chinese Painting*), Abbey Library, London, 1976

Hay, John, *Masterpieces of Chinese Art*, Phaidon Press Ltd, London, 1984

Hejzlar, Josef, *Chinese Watercolours*, Cathay Books, London, 1978

Hillier, J. R., *Japanese Drawings—from the 17th through the 19th Century—Drawings of the Masters*, Little, Brown & Company, Boston and Toronto, 1965

Hirayama, Hakuho, *Sumi-e Just For You—Traditional "One Brush" Ink Painting*, Kodansha International, Ltd, Tokyo, New York and San Francisco, 1979

Ho Huai-Shuo, *Inner Realms of Ho Huai-Shuo*, Hibiya Co., Ltd, Hong Kong, 1981

Hong Kong Museum of Art, *Early Masters of the Lingnam School*, Urban Council of Hong Kong, 1983

Hulton, Paul & Smith, Lawrence, *Flowers in Art from East and West*, British Museum Publications, Ltd, London, 1979

Jenyns, Soame, *A Background to Chinese Painting*, Sidgwick & Jackson, London, 1935, reprinted by Schocken Books, New York, 1966

Lai, T. C., *Chinese Seals*, Kelly & Walsh, Ltd, Hong Kong, 1976
Noble Fragrance—Chinese Flowers & Trees, Swindon Book Company, Kowloon, Hong Kong, 1977

Lao Tsu, *Tao Te Ching*, translated by Gia-Fu Feng & Jane English, Wildwood House, Ltd, London, 1973

Li Chu-tsing, *Trends in Modern Chinese Painting*, Artibus Asiae Publishers, Ascona, Switzerland, 1979

Lin Yutang, *Imperial Chinese Art*, Omega Books, Ware, Hertfordshire, 1961

March, Benjamin, *Some Technical Terms of Chinese Painting*, Paragon Book Reprint Corporation, New York, 1969

Rawson, Philip & Legeza, Laszlo, *Tao—The Chinese Philosophy of Time and Change*, Thames & Hudson, London, 1973

Sickman, Laurence & Soper, Alexander, *The Art and Architecture of China*, The Pelican History of Art, Penguin Books, London, 1956 (reprinted 1978)

Siudzinski, Paul, *Sumi-e: A Meditation in Ink—An Introduction to Japanese Brush Painting*, Sterling Publishing Co., Inc., New York, 1979

Stern, Harold P., *Birds, Beasts, Blossoms, and Bugs—The Nature of Japan*, Harry N. Abrams, Inc., New York, 1976

Sullivan, Michael, *The Meeting of Eastern and Western Art—From the Sixteenth Century to the Present Day*, Thames & Hudson, London, 1973

Chinese Landscape Painting—in the Sui and T'ang Dynasties, University of California Press, Berkeley, 1980

CHINESE
BRUSH
PAINTING

Tregear, Mary, *Chinese Art*, Thames & Hudson, London, 1980

Vedlich, Joseph, *The Prints of the Ten Bamboo Studio*, Crescent Books, Crown Publishers, Inc., New York, 1979

Wang, C. C., *Mountains of the Mind—The Landscapes of C. C. Wang*, Arthur M. Sackler Foundation, Washington DC, 1977

Watson, Professor William (ed.), *The Great Japan Exhibition—Art of the Edo Period 1600–1868*, Royal Academy of Arts catalog, in association with Weidenfeld & Nicolson, London, 1981–1982

Weng Wan-go, *Chinese Painting and Calligraphy*, Dover Publications, Inc., New York, 1978

Whitfield, Roderick, *Five Modern Masters: Chinese Traditional Painting 1886–1966*, Royal Academy of Arts catalog, London, 1982

Williams, C.A.S., *Outlines of Chinese Symbolism and Art Motives*, Dover Publications, Inc., New York, 1976

Wong Kuan S. & Adams, Celeste, *In the Way of the Master—Chinese and Japanese Painting and Calligraphy*, a bulletin of the Museum of Fine Arts, Houston, Texas, NS Volume VII, Number 3, February 1981

Wong Shiu Hon, *Kao Chien-fu's Theory of Painting*, University of Hong Kong, 1972

Wu, Victor (compiler), *Contemporary Chinese Painters 1*, Hai Feng Publishing Co., Hong Kong, 1982

Zhaolina Publishing House, *A Selection of Contemporary Chinese Paintings—From the Collection of Song Wenzhi*, Beijing, 1981

INDEX